PhilanthropyRoundtable

What Comes *Next?*

By Karl Zinsmeister

How private givers can rescue America in an era of political frustration

Published by The Philanthropy Roundtable, 1120 20th Street NW, Suite 550 South, Washington, D.C. 20036

Free copies of this book are available to qualified donors. To learn more, or to order more copies, call (202) 822-8333, e-mail main@PhilanthropyRoundtable.org, or visit PhilanthropyRoundtable.org. Printed and e-book versions are available from major online booksellers. A PDF may be downloaded at no charge at PhilanthropyRoundtable.org.

ISBN 978-0-9861474-8-7
LCCN 2016956012

First printing, November 2016

"The central conservative truth is that it is culture, not politics,
that determines the success of a society.
The central liberal truth is that politics can change a culture."

~Daniel Patrick Moynihan

What Comes Next?

Our political process is parched, harsh, and unproductive. Social disorders are increasing. It seems that life is not getting better. More than two thirds of Americans believe the country is on the wrong track.

Well guess what?

We aren't the first to face this...

Indeed, there have been many such periods in American history.

A key tussle in the Presidential election of 1828 was whose wife was more shameful: Mrs. Jackson or Mrs. Adams. During Jackson's inauguration, observers were amazed at the number of men who ended up with bloody noses. At the White House reception, the crowd broke much of the official china and glassware while pawing their way to the whiskey punch and cake. To avoid being crushed by the mob, the new President had to climb out a ground-floor window. Destruction of the mansion was relieved only when stewards placed tubs of liquor on the front lawn to draw people outside.

There were many violent pastimes in those days, and fighting was common. The two main categories of street disorders were drunken brawls and lynching riots. The lynchers included philanthropists among their targets (note the attacks on the Tappans in my case study on abolition). And the drinkers guzzled *three to four times* as much alcohol per capita as today's consumption (see temperance case study). All of this grog yielded varieties of anarchy we can only begin to fathom, from family abuse to chronic workplace shutdowns due to worker absenteeism.

Yet even in the midst of disheartening social turmoil and dysfunctional politics, good citizens in America never stopped fixing and refining our society. When it was almost impossible to make progress through government, men and women poured their energy and money into repairing our culture in other ways: through charity, voluntary associations, mass movements, business innovations, and grassroots action.

And I don't just mean clubs that bought flagpoles for the town square. Many of the most consequential reforms accomplished in America—finding inventive fixes to problems that cast dark shadows over our future, problems that had stumped all levels of government—were the products of direct citizen action. The four case studies attached to this essay show in detail how thousands of spontaneous private efforts took the raw edges off nineteenth-century America and set our nation up for modern success. It was not political activity but rather private organizing that:

- Brought literacy to the half of our democracy locked in ignorance.
- Moderated our terrible national drinking problem.
- Turned Americans against the stain of slavery.
- Tamed the cultural fractures, crime, and community breakdown produced by massive foreign immigration, industrialization, and dislocation of small-town residents into big cities.
- Elevated individual character through religious revival and self-improvement crusades that defined what we now think of as the quintessential American values.

You will also read in this essay about more recent civil organizing that continues to solve or soften our most distressing contemporary problems—often in sectors where government officials have repeatedly swung and missed.

It's a reality that U.S. politics is likely to be a source of frustration for some years to come. But even if elections remain a cruel blood sport, and government agencies continue to be ineffective at addressing the key maladies that afflict us, and Washington, D.C., remains frozen tundra for people who want to improve America, there is no reason to be depressed, to abandon public life, to doubt our nation's ability to make progress. There are many paths to progress other than those that run along

Andrew Jackson's inauguration was a festival of drunkenness, fistfights, and disorder. Much of the White House china and glassware was destroyed as visitors clawed at the food and drink. The President-elect was nearly crushed by the rowdy crowd at one point, and to draw the mob out of the mansion stewards had to position tubs of whiskey punch outside on the lawn.

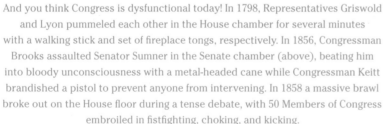

And you think Congress is dysfunctional today! In 1798, Representatives Griswold and Lyon pummeled each other in the House chamber for several minutes with a walking stick and set of fireplace tongs, respectively. In 1856, Congressman Brooks assaulted Senator Sumner in the Senate chamber (above), beating him into bloody unconsciousness with a metal-headed cane while Congressman Keitt brandished a pistol to prevent anyone from intervening. In 1858 a massive brawl broke out on the House floor during a tense debate, with 50 Members of Congress embroiled in fistfighting, choking, and kicking.

the Potomac, many precedents and prior triumphs we can copy, many productive places where good citizens can invest themselves in making America finer.

So there is no reason to jump on the bandwagon and practice politics as full-blown warfare on fellow citizens, to retreat into private affairs, into moneymaking alone, into simply maximizing outcomes for our own families or our own communities. While private success is the foundation for all public service, withdrawing into parochial concerns is never good for a nation.

If you are a successful, public-spirited American disappointed by today's political possibilities, you should consider pouring yourself into savvy philanthropy and working the levers of civil society to solve gnawing problems. Get out there and give money, volunteer elbow grease, and invest talent in fixing the problems that afflict us as a people. This can be done in many ways, in almost any sector of society, in every one of our communities. And successful small efforts are as important as big ones. The key is simply to succeed. To change. To educate. To build human competence and end sadness. To triumph over illness and poverty and antisocial behavior and false values. There are literally millions of wide-open fields yawning for leaders.

This kind of organizing and acting and spending for high purposes—entirely outside of the political process—has happened many times before in our country, including in eras when the national prospects were considerably bleaker than they are now. Millions of patriotic Americans have found effective and satisfying ways other than politics to move culture and opinion and social practice. It can happen again.

Been there, done that

Here's a picture for you: Demagogues and pundits have abandoned serious discussion of principles and stooped to slanders, falsehood, trickery, and the "scalping and roasting alive" of opponents. These cheap tricks have aroused "low passions" among the public, and "wild, blind reckless partisanship" is overtaking reason and individual judgment. Scholars say no other era was more politically fractured and obsessed with ideology.

Many Americans are shocked by the crudeness of public discourse, and by unprecedented eruptions of vulgarity in daily life. Substance abuse is on the rise, particularly among the working class, which is thought to be under serious stress due to national economic dislocations. There is alarm over the levels of waste and fraud taking place in government, at the national as well as state and local levels. Racial antagonism and scapegoating have resulted in violence and street clashes with authorities in places stretching from Ohio to New York to Missouri, plunging some cities into what observers call "mobocracy."

Seem familiar? What you have just read is a description, from mournful contemporary reports, of Jacksonian America. In the first half of the 1800s, many people felt there was something going profoundly wrong in the U.S. Millions pined for thoroughgoing reform.

One impressive young attorney warned a Midwestern audience in 1838 that "There is something of ill-omen amongst us. I mean the increasing disregard for law which pervades the country; the growing disposition to substitute the wild and furious passions in lieu of the sober judgment." That young lawyer was named Abraham Lincoln.

Our country was groping blindly, roughly, raggedly to figure out how to function as the world's first mass democracy. A remarkably talented, principled, and comparatively selfless group of political leaders had risen up to lead our nation to independence, but the Washingtons and Madisons had now passed on, and we were settling in for the long slog. A brand new party system—including the idea that winners of elections earned the right to stuff the government with their cronies, and often their pockets with silver—was taking hold at every level of politics, from the national capital to Tammany Hall. This was an era of fraud, embezzlement, and self-enrichment at the public trough.

Elections turned into circuses. Votes were openly traded for booze, jobs, or favors. One South Carolinian observed that "civilization" retreats more in one month before an election than it can advance in six months afterward. A Presidential election was "a national calamity" in its effects on public morals.

Sensitive citizens decried "the evils of party spirit" that tore through our politics. Many retreated to quixotic alternatives like the Antimasonic Party or the Liberty Party. If you think we live in a partisan world now, consider this description by a Tennessean of U.S. life in the mid-1800s: "The hotels, the stores, and even the shops were regarded as Whig or Democratic, and thus patronized by the parties. There was scarcely any such thing as neutrality. Almost every one— high or low, rich or poor, black or white—was arranged on one side or the other."

Parts of our culture other than politics also frequently frayed and split—geographic regions, religious denominations, organs of journalism, central-bank vs. no-bank businessmen. Ethnicity and social class were sore points as millions of new immigrants started to flood into the U.S., bringing patterns of religious practice, family structure, alcohol use,

It's a reality that U.S. politics is likely to be a source of frustration for some years to come. But even if Washington, D.C., remains frozen tundra for people who want to improve America, there is no reason to doubt our nation's ability to make progress.

A barnraising. A maple-syrup bee. Church-building. Mutual aid among neighbors was solving problems in American communities long before there were duly constituted agencies of the state. This genius for joining together informally continues to be our deepest strength.

work, and home life that were unfamiliar and often unwelcome. This was exacerbated by the surge of rural men and women pulled out of small towns by industrialization and urbanism. Farm boys "poured into the city to mingle with Irish immigrants, all looking for work and mostly finding crime, slums, whiskey, and poverty," comments one historian.

Harsh schisms separated Americans. Baleful influences were corrupting the character of individual citizens. And our government entities were not effective at turning any of this around.

The exhaustion of politics

These are not the kinds of problems that politics and policy changes can cure. In many of these cases, politics was the *cause* of the illness. So savvy cultural leaders, businessmen, preachers, and even wise government officials increasingly turned away from policies and government programs and elections as panaceas, and started looking for other ways to fix what ailed America. It became clear that the European tradition of using politics to restrain and control anarchic lower classes, which the Federalists and Democrats had also dabbled with early in the life of our nation, was not viable in America.

Soon "it was no longer as fashionable as it had been for businessmen to enter the sometimes dirty game of politics," writes historian Bertram Wyatt-Brown. Instead, many of them put their patriotic energies and money behind private organizations created to lift up fellow citizens. Education, moral striving, and self-improvement became the watchwords, and "the associative principle was approached with a new intensity." An explosion of groups burst forth to teach people how to read, what to feed a baby, means of saving money, how to understand the Bible, ways to keep a house sanitary, reasons to avoid alcohol and tobacco, how to find a job, when to discipline children, where to donate to others less well-off than you, and myriad other socially valuable behaviors.

The society that our founders aimed to create was one that enshrined both freedom and goodness, notes author Richard Cornuelle:

We wanted, from the beginning, a free society, free in the sense that every man was his own supervisor and the architect of his own ambitions…. We wanted as well, with equal fervor, a good society—a humane, responsible society in which helping hands reached out to people in honest distress, in which common needs were met.... We created a much wider variety of new institutions for this purpose than we built to insure political freedom. As a frontier people, accustomed to interdependence, we developed a genius for solving common problems. People joined together in bewildering combinations to found schools, churches, opera houses, co-ops, hospitals, to build bridges and canals, to help the poor. To see a need was, more often than not, to promote a scheme to meet it better than had ever been done before.

This dual devotion to liberty and goodness defined the American project and allowed it to succeed brilliantly. It needs to be kept in mind, though, that there were no other democracies around for early Americans to learn from. We had to figure out how to make rule-by-the-ordinary work, and most Americans felt the fragility of our experiment—and the need to constantly repeat the processes of education, moral striving, and societal and self improvement.

Inner reform redeems culture

While the health of a radically self-governing country like ours depends upon the moral decency and wisdom of rank-and-file residents, the state must rely on other parts of society—families, churches, charities and organs of philanthropy—to build up that inner goodness. Recognizing this paradox, and the potential danger to our republic, generations of American leaders poured themselves into bolstering and building the virtue-creating institutions of civil society. They did this with dual goals in sight: They wanted to elevate individual character, and to gentle some of the cruder aspects of our collective culture. "From individual regeneration and social stability would come national progress," is how one observer put it.

French artist Jacques Milbert drew this image of a Methodist camp meeting in 1819. Clergy, evangelical donors, and millions of reborn believers powered dramatic change in personal behavior and social life in what historians call our Second Great Awakening.

It was much easier to do this during periods of religious revival. Our First Great Awakening, rippling through what were still colonies, cemented in American minds the idea that every person is a sovereign being with full status before God. That set the stage for our political revolution based on the proposition that "All men are created equal."

What historians call America's Second Great Awakening rose and peaked during the first half of the nineteenth century. It brought mass understanding that each person is responsible for perfecting his soul as much as possible, and for lifting up his neighbor whenever he is able. In this way the Second Great Awakening paved the way for a moral revolution as profound as

> **What happens in our hearts, in our families, and in our interactions with our direct neighbors is far more important in shaping our future prospects (and the collective course of our nation) than most of what unfolds in our politics, our policies, or our laws.**

our political revolution—one that accomplished tremendous things like ending slavery, universalizing literacy, and cementing across our middle class what we now think of as the classic American virtues. Qualities like neighborliness, honesty, hard work, self-discipline, thrift, and sobriety were nowhere near omnipresent in Jacksonian America. The fact that they are admired as norms today is a product of the evangelical campaigns that roared across America starting in the early 1800s.

The men and women who slayed demon rum, broke slaves' shackles, cleaned up the tenements, taught illiterate European peasants and freed blacks to read, and rooted the golden rule in American breasts did so by translating religious commitment into social improvement. Theirs is a fascinating tale, with relevance in many places to our contemporary circumstances. Be sure to read the case studies on the Second Great Awakening and on the remarkable Sunday Schooling movement that transformed America in so many ways.

There is no mistaking the fact that these evangelical reformers were direct heirs of our Puritan tradition. One of the philanthropic heroes of the Second Great Awakening (and a recurring figure in the case studies) was Lewis Tappan. A letter sent by his mother-in-law to his wife provides a representative, and amusing, glimpse of the strong internal restraint that the Protestant ethic nurtured within Americans during this era. These motherly instructions were offered to the not-yet-married daughter while she was visiting a friend in a nearby city:

- *Be cautious of speaking about any person.*
  (This is good Christian counsel discouraging gossip.)
- *Put your trust where it can never be disappointed.*
  (For those of you who didn't have evangelical mothers—this is code.)
- *Don't go out in the evening.*
  (Blatant code.)
- *Keep near your friend Miss Smith.*
  (More strong code.)
- *Write me <u>immediately</u> if you have been dancing.*
  (Foundational dogma of both the Methodist and Baptist churches.)

The social reformers of our Second Great Awakening firmly believed that self-discipline is the key to success, happiness, and good citizenship. What happens in our hearts, in our families, and in our interactions with our neighbors, they insisted, is far more important in shaping our future prospects (and the collective course of our nation) than most of what happens in politics, policy, or law.

That perspective continues to have strong relevance. In their book *Good Faith*, authors David Kinnaman and Gabe Lyons suggest that in 2016 America "we are engaged in a struggle over the human imagination." On one side is a view that says self-fulfillment and personal pleasure are what matter. You only live once. Grab as many good feelings as you can. On the other side is an ancient view that says, actually, the point of life is to redeem, restore, and continually re-create yourself into an ever-higher state (even when that's unpleasurable) while simultaneously pulling along as many other human beings as you can. We need to refine our own souls, love others, and build a better culture.

That latter view was the ethic that made America both a free society and a good society during our first century after independence. Facing problems similar to today's but far more widespread, our American predecessors managed to dramatically transform our culture within one generation. Many astonishing details are provided in the case studies later in this book.

These predecessors used all the tools of civil society and grassroots action: New technologies enabled persuasion via mass communication. Music and novels and other elements of popular culture were deployed to grab people's hearts. Hundreds of thousands of passionate young-adult volunteers were recruited; they developed potent role-modeling and mentoring relationships with needy children just a decade or two younger, inspiring them to change their lives. Powerful legal interventions established new precedents in the courts. Schools, churches, and fraternal clubs were created in barren spots. Reporters were cleverly wooed. Good citizenship, neighborliness, and national unity were cultivated in myriad ways. New concepts of work, leisure, and self-improvement were fostered, turning Americans into constant tinkerers and re-inventors—not just of machinery, but of their own souls.

All of these things have been done in America. They were achieved, not so long ago, through strong leadership from donors, social entrepreneurs, and philanthropists of all stripes. Similar things can be done today.

Good citizens don't just consume governance; they produce it

Keep in mind that civil society, volunteer help, and charitable assistance sprang up in the U.S. even before government did. In most of our new communities, mutual aid among neighbors was solving problems long before there were duly constituted agencies of the state. When the French observer Alexis de Tocqueville studied America's rich tradition of voluntary action almost 200 years ago, what impressed him was not just its ability to meet practical needs, but the way it exercised and strengthened the social muscles required for people to govern

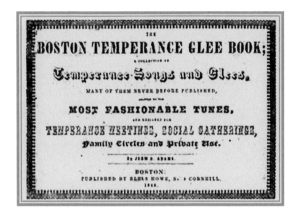

Determined to build large, popular, influential movements, social reformers made room for fun, sociability, and "glee" in their activities.

themselves in a healthy republic. Tocqueville believed that the many charities and civic groups operating across the U.S. were not just signs but ultimately the *source* of effective self-rule.

Widespread involvement in societies created to solve local problems "fosters a taste for liberty among the people, and teaches them the art of being free," summarized Tocqueville. An "American learns about the law by participating in the making of it. He teaches himself about the forms of government by governing. He watches the great work of society being done every day before his eyes, and, in a sense, by his hand…. So feeble and limited is the share of government left to the administration…it is fair to say that the people govern themselves."

It isn't just the mechanics of democratic rule that develop in this way. Empathy for other citizens also grows out of the personal contact of civic association. "Feelings and ideas are renewed, the heart enlarged, and understanding developed only by the reciprocal action of men upon another," says Tocqueville.

Edmund Burke also viewed local associations as the nursery for broader loyalty to one's fellow man. "The little platoon we belong to in society is the first principle (the germ as it were) of public affections. It is the first link in the series by which we proceed towards a love to our country, and to mankind," he wrote.

> Allowing people to vote every couple years on whether to change a few members of a class of full-time politicians ruling over us is *not* American-style self-rule.

Jefferson promoted a style of governance "where every man is a sharer in the direction of his ward-republic…and feels that he is a participant in the government of affairs, not merely at election one day in the year, but every day." This is not just theory, but the way America was set up to operate, and the way it came to thrive.

So that's our history. What about now? Writer John McClaughry warns that today "we are steadily reducing the scope of local civic responsibility." When we insist on professionalizing and centralizing all social problem-solving in government, we fall into the trap that Jefferson warned against: "concentrating all cares into one body." Allowing people to vote every couple years on whether to change a few members of a class of full-time politicians ruling over us is *not* American-style self-rule.

"This is the issue: whether we believe in our capacity for self-government, or whether we abandon the American Revolution and confess that a little intellectual elite in a far-distant capital can plan our lives for us better than we can plan them ourselves." That was how

Ronald Reagan put it in one of his classic speeches. When we transfer responsibility for strengthening our communities away from the direct-democracy of civil society and charity and voluntary action, and toward bureaucratic agencies instead, we don't just get clumsier, more impersonal services—we *shrink the arena of American citizenship*, as McClaughry puts it. That is a crucial reason so many Americans now feel alienated from government and politics.

And for all of this, philanthropic action is a perfect antidote. You can think of the millions and millions of private givers and volunteers in our country, and the hundreds of thousands of nonprofit organizations, as a kind of matrix of private legislatures. They define social ills, set goals and priorities for attacking them, then methodically marshal money and labor toward solutions. And philanthropic Americans do all this spontaneously—without asking the state's permission. When we do these things we become *producers of governance* rather than just *consumers* of government. We take direct action to improve the life around us instead of being dependent citizens who wait for officials to descend as saviors.

Philanthropy and government

Enlightened, practical, democratic leaders shouldn't just tolerate the independent actions of donors and volunteers, they should encourage them. Social entrepreneur Neerav Kingsland, who gained prominence by helping build the nation's most extensive web of independent charter schools in New Orleans after Hurricane Katrina, has argued that the most effective and humane thing that many public servants can do today to help needy populations is to let go of their monopolies on power. He uses the term "Relinquishers" to describe progress-minded officials who are willing to transfer authority away from centralized bureaucracies in order

Neerav Kingsland, CEO of the Hastings Fund established by Netflix CEO Reed Hastings to improve schools.

to allow experimentation and improvement driven by philanthropy, commerce, grassroots activism, and other independent forces.

As an example of how quickly societal conditions can improve when intelligent Relinquishers cede power to civil actors, consider the events that unfolded in New Orleans after philanthropists were allowed to pour resources and expertise into restructuring that city's schools following the Katrina disaster. Government continued to provide funds, fair rules, and accountability, but it allowed independent operators launched with philanthropic seed-funding to take over the running of academies. The result was that the number of classroom seats rated "high-quality" quadrupled in four years. The proportion of ninth graders graduating on time four years later leapt from 54 to 73 percent. The fraction of students showing adequate proficiency on state tests doubled. The ACT scores of graduating seniors hit an historic high.

If ceding or sharing responsibility for societal improvement with funders and volunteers in civil society will often be the most practical path to success—as well as the more democratic course—why do some government authorities resist it?

Tyrants hate philanthropy for obvious reasons. In countries like Russia, China, and Iran, charities are regularly shut down out of fear that they'll provide solutions and social legitimacy outside of the state. Only the freest societies have had flourishing philanthropic sectors. In America, our freedom to make charitable interventions without supervision or control is ultimately sheltered by the First Amendment of our Bill of Rights, which protects our right to assemble and act outside of government, to dissent, to take heterogeneous, unpopular, or minority-supported action to redress grievances.

But even in free countries like the U.S., there are many officials who prefer that everyday citizens be consumers of government rather than producers of governance through their own actions. Other than in the first week of November they want us to stay home and leave refinement of American society to "the experts." Most politicians, in both parties, proceed as if our country has only two problem-solving sectors: the public sector of government and the private sector of business. They ignore the third sector that operates in the space between the coercion of law and the profit-seeking of commerce, between the isolated individual and the impersonal state.

WORLD

Russia's Putin Signs New Law Against 'Undesirable' NGOs

Legislation gives authorities power to shut down foreign and international organizations

Governments in autocratic nations routinely clamp down on philanthropy. But even in free countries, many officials would prefer that citizens passively consume governance rather than produce it on their own.

Philanthropy and government are often competitors in serving the public welfare, and Americans who prefer that society be steered from a central position frequently resist philanthropic solutions. In some quarters, "the very idea of competition with government is, by a weird public myth, thought to be illegitimate, disruptive, divisive, unproductive, and perhaps immoral," writes Richard Cornuelle. That, he warns, is a mistake.

Far from being illegitimate, lively competition with government is essential if our democratic institutions are to work sensibly.... The government doesn't ignore public opinion because the people who run it are naturally perverse. It isn't wasteful because it is manned by wasteful people.... Without competition, the bureaucracy can't make government efficient.... Innovation painfully disrupts its way of life. Reform comes only through competitive outsiders who force steady efficient adjustment to changing situations.

Outside resistance isn't the only obstacle. Advocates of voluntary action themselves sometimes get lazy or timid. Philanthropy "must

As we transfer responsibility for strengthening our communities away from the direct democracy of civil society, charity, and voluntary action, and toward bureaucratic agencies instead, we don't just get clumsier, more impersonal services—*we shrink the arena of American citizenship.* That is a crucial reason so many Americans today feel alienated from government and politics.

be as eager as government to take on new public problems," urges Cornuelle. "Its unique indispensable natural role in America is to compete with government."

Government is important but can't rescue us on its own

Obviously we don't expect or want government to entirely wither away. There's scant chance of that in any case! All modern trends are in the direction of state bloat and an increasingly heavy tread from public entities.

But it is foolish to expect that government is going to ride to the rescue of our culture. Government is not becoming more effective today. It is not growing nimbler. It is not zeroing in on our central stresses and weaknesses.

So philanthropy should. And can. Scads of social improvements have been instigated by philanthropy while government was AWOL. In recent years, philanthropists have stepped into many breaches in performance by public agencies and offered repairs.

- It is philanthropy and civil society that sparked real and desperately needed education reform, providing the most helpful new ideas of the last generation for improving public education. Examples include charter schools, Teach For America, hard-headed teacher assessment and accountability, value-added pay, potent new STEM programs, widened access to school choice, revived religious and private schools for needy children, enriched digital-learning options, and much more.
- Donors jumped obstacles to improve the management of many neglected or mishandled medical conditions like autism, breast and prostate cancer, Ebola, and schizophrenia.
- Givers inaugurated the Green Revolution, attacked tropical diseases, invented and spread microlending, promoted individual land ownership for peasants, and shielded entrepreneurs from government stultification in order to reduce misery in developing countries.
- Philanthropy has revived hundreds of ill-maintained urban parks that millions of Americans depend on to refresh themselves (beginning with Central Park in New York City), and is creating many dramatically new and popular parks in underserved areas of

Houston, Atlanta, Chicago, Tulsa, Dallas, Memphis, Louisville, and other cities.

- It is philanthropy and civil society that recently invented new approaches to chronic problems in the U.S. like foster care and adoption backlogs, drunk driving, health relapses among elderly patients just released from hospitals, addictions to smoking/drugs/alcohol, various stall-outs in medical innovation, and so forth.

- Amidst gross underperformance by government job-training programs, philanthropy is strengthening the ability of community colleges to transform manual workers into middle-skill employees with technical and service capacities that are 1) badly needed by our economy, and 2) paid wages that will support a family at a middle-class level.

- At research universities, donors have been crucial in birthing important new fields like biomedical engineering, computer-assisted learning, gerontology, character and leadership education, systems biology, and so forth—frequently after battling through serious resistance from government and other bureaucracies.

- Even when it comes to getting government's own house in order in the form of repairing today's dangerous trillion-dollar underfunding of public-pension systems, it is philanthropists who have guided political leaders to constructive win-win solutions in locales ranging from Rhode Island to Detroit to Utah.

Julius Rosenwald donated money and organizing that built nearly 5,000 schools for African-American children whose education was being neglected by the state.

For concrete suggestions on successes that might be added in the future to the roster of philanthropic assists to American governance, see the subsection "A wish list for next steps" a few pages ahead.

It's not wise to rely solely on government

Be aware that jealous, controlling politicians will often resist an assertive charitable sector. Many are reluctant to share responsibilities with civil society and private associations. Few elected officials have any idea of how important philanthropy has been to the process of social invention in America.

"Every single great idea that has marked the twenty-first century, the twentieth century, and the nineteenth century has required government vision and government incentive," said Vice President Joe Biden recently. "The ballot box is the place where all change begins in America," insisted Senator Ted Kennedy.

People with this view overlook the potent accomplishments of private giving throughout American history. (See this essay's case studies, and the 1,340 pages of the recently published *Almanac of American Philanthropy*, for an abundance of examples.) They also ignore the *dangers* of relying solely on government as an agent of reform.

Advocates who would have you believe that no good social change happens unless the government engineers it like to cite the civil rights movement as a favorite example. Is that accurate? Let's look at the actual forces that ended second-class citizenship in the U.S.

You can think of the millions and millions of private givers and volunteers in our country, and the hundreds of thousands of nonprofit organizations, as a kind of matrix of private legislatures. They define social ills, set goals and priorities for executing them, then methodically marshal money and labor toward solutions.

Back in 1704—when 1,500 African Americans in New York City were held in bondage with full government sanction, and educating them was forbidden, private donors set up schools to instruct hundreds of slaves on the quiet. In the early 1830s, when state and federal governments still made it a crime to teach a slave to read, private donors like Arthur Tappan were paying for African Americans to go to college. In 1865, the donor-funded American Missionary Association put 350 agents in the field and invested the modern equivalent of several hundred million dollars to protect newly emancipated slaves from vengeful mobs and help them buy emergency rations, find land to settle on, marry legally, and put their children in schools. The AMA also chartered and privately funded eight academies that became the core of what are now referred to as America's historically black colleges and universities.

Less than two years after the bullets of the Civil War stopped flying, philanthropist George Peabody was distributing millions of his own dollars across the South to train teachers and set up schools without racial considerations so that freed slaves and other illiterates could get learning—despite the ferocious antipathy of state and local governments for that cause. In 1891, philanthropist Katharine Drexel gave her entire fortune (half a billion dollars in contemporary terms) to create a new religious order devoted to assisting blacks and Native Americans. She established 50 schools for African Americans, 145 missions and 12 schools for Native Americans, plus the black college Xavier University in New Orleans. In these same years, governments at all levels were doing little more than breaking promises to Native Americans and neglecting African Americans.

As the twentieth century opened, hundreds of governments were fiercely enforcing Jim Crow laws that stunted the education of blacks. But John Rockefeller was pouring money into his new effort to provide primary education to African Americans. Then he boosted up 1,600 new high schools for blacks and poor whites. He eventually put almost $325 million of his personal fortune into the venture. Simultaneously he was spending millions to improve the health and daily productivity of poor blacks and whites by nearly eliminating the hookworm that was then endemic in rural areas.

Numerous private givers followed the leads of Tappan, Peabody, Drexel, and Rockefeller and donated millions of dollars to improve the education and social status of African Americans at a time when they had no friends in government. Philanthropic help came from Anna Jeanes's Negro Rural Schools Fund, the Phelps Stokes Fund, the Virginia Randolph Fund, the John Slater Fund, and legions of individuals. These continued their work until government finally caught up and started desegregating schools in the 1960s.

African-American youngsters whose education and social conditions were being wholly neglected by the state got their biggest lift of all from philanthropist Julius Rosenwald. Starting in 1912, he donated the current equivalent of billions of dollars to build schoolhouses in hundreds of counties where black education was ignored. In less than 20 years, the Rosenwald program erected 4,977 rural schools and 380 companion community buildings in most of America's locales with a substantial black population. At the time of Rosenwald's death in 1932, the schools he built were educating fully 27 percent of all the African-American children in our country.

Many economic producers and sensible leaders graduated from these philanthropic schools. Absent those private efforts by donors, racial improvement and reconciliation in our country would have been delayed by generations. Government not only had little to do with this philanthropic uplift—many arms of government did their very best to resist or obstruct it.

That's not ancient history

A skeptic might say, "Well that's nice, but it's ancient history. Today, the government leads all necessary reform of this sort." That is gravely mistaken.

Guess where America's most segregated and often most inadequate government-run schools are located at present? All in northern cities with activist governments (like Detroit, Milwaukee, New York, Newark, Chicago, and Philadelphia), according to research by the U.C.L.A. Civil Rights Project and others. In inner-city schools, a third to a half of all minority students fail to graduate from high school, and the academic competence of even those who do graduate is grossly below the national standard. Enormous commitments of effort and money to conventional government-run schools over the last 25 years have brought hardly any progress against these failures.

The one place where education has clearly improved for inner-city children over the last generation is charter schools. In 25 years, donors and social entrepreneurs have seeded about 7,000 charters in some of the neediest parts of the U.S.

There is just one place where education has clearly improved in inner cities: charter schooling. About 7,000 charter schools (and rising fast) have been seeded across the U.S. by donors and social entrepreneurs, starting from zero 25 years ago. Two thirds of charter-school students are minorities, and half are extremely low-income. Yet Stanford researchers and other investigators find that these children are receiving significantly better educations than counterparts in conventional government-run schools, in some cases outscoring comfortable suburban schools in annual testing. Families have voted with their feet, pulling millions of their children from conventional government-run schools. More languish on the long waiting lists created by artificially capped school numbers, inequitable funding, and other means some public officials have used to obstruct expansion of the most important social invention of the last generation for American children.

Or let's look at another area where conventional wisdom says progress can be made only under governmental banners: saving refugees of war.

Fred Cuny was a larger-than-life Texas engineer and charitable entrepreneur who used money donated by George Soros to save lives in Bosnia more effectively than all the material assistance offered by national governments plus the U.N. *combined.*

When we take direct action to improve the life around us, instead of waiting for officials to descend as saviors, we become *producers of governance* rather than just *consumers* of government.

When in 1915 Ottomans launched a genocide against Armenian Christians that ultimately took 1.5 million lives, the U.S. government did little. But everyday Americans, missionaries, church members, and philanthropists sprang into action to both save lives and then sustain survivors. Nearly 1,000 Americans volunteered to go to the region to build orphanages and help refugees. They assumed responsibility for 130,000 mother- and fatherless children, and rescued more than a million adults.

When at about that same time the U.S. Ambassador to the Ottoman Empire discovered that Jews in Palestine were starving to death, his urgent telegram went to philanthropist Jacob Schiff in New York rather than to Washington. A fundraising committee was set up, and over the next few years it distributed hundreds of millions of dollars, donated by more than 3 million private givers, protecting many thousands of Jews.

It was a similar story when fascism swept Europe. The U.S. government dragged its feet and failed to organize any competent effort to save the Jews, gypsies, Christians, and others targeted by the Nazis. Private donors jumped into the breach. The Rockefeller Foundation, for instance, established two special funds that worked, under the most difficult wartime conditions, to relocate mortally endangered individuals to Allied countries.

As with our civil-rights example, philanthropy taking up crucial overseas burdens in the face of government failure is not just a story in the past tense. In 1993, all Western governments were pathetically slow and inadequate in their response to the ethnic cleansing in Bosnia that killed tens of thousands. The most effective actor by far was philanthropist George Soros—who used $50 million of his own money to insert a highly capable relief team into the city of Sarajevo while it was under siege, re-establishing gas and electric service during the bitter winter, setting up an alternate water supply, and bringing in desperately needed provisions. It has been estimated that Soros's gift saved more lives than the on-the-ground interventions of all national governments plus the United Nations *combined.*

A wish list for next steps

Again, this is not a call to give up efforts to improve our government and political process. Patriotic Americans will always work for a better public sector and healthy politics. But efforts at government improvement proceed at glacial rates—and regularly retreat backward. While those back-and-forth attempts at good government unfold, philanthropy can make many real-life improvements in America.

Where might you as a social entrepreneur make a contribution, starting almost immediately? Many exciting initiatives are already incubating and could be expanded quickly by enlightened philanthropists. Others are ripe for the founding. Here are some practical suggestions on where leaders of civil society could be enormously helpful to America over the next decade or so, if they will put their minds, shoulders, and checkbooks to the task:

- An urgent attack is needed on **drug addiction** using modern tools of science, pharmacology, social reinforcement, faith, and economics. Donors could also inaugurate sophisticated new campaigns against the precursors that lead to addiction among vulnerable populations.

- Speaking of new, what's preventing tech-oriented philanthropists from launching a large collaborative crusade to reduce today's dire weaknesses in **cybersecurity**? Many of the ugly privacy breaches and worrying security holes in our computer webs are just a result of out-of-date procedures and tools, and a shortage of understanding. As can be attested by anyone who has seen the antique technology on display in Social Security offices, FAA control towers, or police stations, government is usually the last sector where advanced computer standards arrive. But a mix of nonprofit organizations and private companies could research this yawning problem, establish consensus on common standards, and lead the way toward less hackability and fallibility in the IT networks on which so much of our personal and national lives now depend.

- America desperately needs a bloom of creative services that can stop the rocketing rise of **single-parent childrearing**—which is seriously damaging the well-being of our next generation of American children, and feeding the tumorous growth of many secondary social pathologies. Unlike a generation ago when Americans sensed this was a problem but had no idea how to reverse it, we are now getting research and embryonic field experimentation, including from The Philanthropy Roundtable's

Culture of Freedom Initiative, that donors can build on to find lasting solutions to family decay.

- Vigorous **Americanization** efforts that provide immigrants with accelerated language training, computer literacy, higher job skills, family coaching, and citizenship instruction could speed the success and integration of this last generation's large bulge of new arrivals—many of whom live and work with awkward separations from other Americans, creating unease on all sides. This is work that thousands of philanthropists energetically threw themselves into in previous American eras—with enormous success—so we needn't wonder whether this is an undertaking that lends itself to civil-society solutions. It does.

- Another sector where civil society has proven it can make progress (and where government is utterly disqualified from even trying to help) is in rebuilding the **religious participation** of Americans. Within the last decade or two we have entered onto a steep and slippery downward slope when it comes to the practice of faith—with many negative ramifications for community intactness, mutual aid, generosity to others, rates of volunteering, and the inculcation of healthy habits that help individuals resist destructive personal behaviors. The sky is the limit on ways donors could help. How about bolstering today's most effective seminaries (just as donors have expanded our most effective K-12 teacher-training programs)? How about rotating capital funds to help burgeoning churches that often now perch in rented sanctuaries, suburban office parks, high-school auditoriums, or strip malls buy the inspiring but nearly empty and moldering buildings of ghost congregations in cities, creating exciting physical campuses where muscular religious practice and healing can be revived where they are most needed? How about just doing a better job of letting people know what's available? In one recent test in Dayton, Ohio, through the Culture of Freedom Initiative, donors were able to increase church attendance at 110 participating congregations by applying sophisticated market research and microtargeting.

- One of the most troubling trends in our welfare state today is the soaring rate at which prime-age individuals are enrolling in

23

> The 1980s brought efforts to shift some authority from Washington to state and local governments. Nothing wrong with that, but what I am proposing here is much more thoroughgoing—lots of tasks should be shifted out of government altogether and handed off to the organs of civil society.

permanent **disability** programs. Millions are dropping out of the productive workforce to depend on easy but dribbling public payments that often leave them not only economically hand-to-mouth but also socially disconnected and personally depressed. Over the last generation we've undergone medical, technological, and legal revolutions that make it possible for almost anyone to contribute to society—it's just a matter of finding the right match of job abilities, needs, and accommodations. But so far we've wasted these new opportunities to integrate people with disabilities into mainstream self-support. Inventive philanthropists could have an enormous influence in rolling back today's troubling surge of Americans languishing on disability. Some donors already are, like those backing the Independence Project now being run by HireHeroesUSA to transform injured veterans into proudly independent workers instead of government dependents. There is an enormous upside for more work like this.

- More generally, the nonprofit sector needs to lead a push to **train and re-train** the large number of Americans who have dropped out of the labor force, are stuck in jobs that can't support their families, or are clinging by their fingernails to positions likely to disappear in the future. Our modern economy requires a culture of lifelong learning and regular skill-burnishing, yet government agencies have a dismal record at these tasks. Nonprofit organizations, however, have showed real verve in figuring out how to train economic strugglers, as documented in two recent guidebooks from The Philanthropy Roundtable (*Clearing Obstacles to Work,* and *Learning to Be Useful*). An expansion of these tailored job-training efforts, which transform the lives of men and women missed by state programs, would be an enormous public service.
- We need new approaches to **homelessness** that treat the whole person, combining material and therapeutic supports with a tough-love approach that expects and requires from the beneficiary personal investment and change.
- The pioneering work that has been done in Colorado, Georgia, and other states showing that backlogs of children languishing in **foster care** can be radically reduced needs to be transferred to scores of other states and expanded, with philanthropic investment, bringing much more wholesome family life to hundreds of thousands of threatened boys and girls.
- Today's nascent efforts to provide mentoring, job services, family bolstering, church support, and housing help to individuals who are **leaving prison** need to be scaled up dramatically. Millions of convicted persons will be returning to our communities over the next decade. Whether they become assets, burdens, or predators is to some considerable degree up to us as neighbors.

Philanthropy's bandwidth is increasing

These are all prime targets for philanthropic intervention. In many of these areas, there are reasons to believe not only that civil society can succeed, but that civil society is the *only* entity that has a fighting chance to make permanent progress against these afflictions. While they are gearing up new ventures like those I've suggested above, some philanthropists have asked me whether they might need to throttle back a bit on overseas aid, arts grants, university funding, and other kinds of good work in order to free up some resources and managerial bandwidth. I believe such funding could be moderated for a period of time, without undue harm, to open up space for fresh and urgently needed culture reform. Ultimately, though, each donor must make that decision for him- or herself.

There is good reason to believe that philanthropy can do more than it is today without requiring drastic zero-sum cuts to existing efforts. For one thing, charitable giving has been stuck at about 2 percent of GDP for many decades. Discretionary income and standards of living have risen dramatically over that same time, so there is room for increased giving without personal pain.

And the personalization revolution now sweeping modern society is giving donors new ways to succeed. Localized solutions, case-by-case variation of social services, relying on trial-and-error tests to see what works—these are longstanding strengths of charitable problem-solving (as I'll touch on in the subsection "Centerless self-rule" just ahead). In a personalized, crowdsourced, decentralized, sharing economy, philanthropy is well positioned to thrive. As valuable as it has been in the past, there is reason to believe private giving can be even more useful for fixing social glitches in the future.

Especially since the charitable sector is advancing fast in mechanics. Charities are taking up powerful new tools and improving traditional methods. Bold efforts are now bringing the power of the profit motive, practical techniques from business, the creative energy of entrepreneurship, and the cool discipline of investment strategy to philanthropic projects. There are many exciting innovations in form: investments and loans where once there were just grants, openness to charitable work done through LLCs, better tracking and assessment, more giving by individuals instead of just foundations, more young donors.

In "applying investment and business tools to social problems," argues venture-capitalist Ronald Cohen, "we are on the verge of a

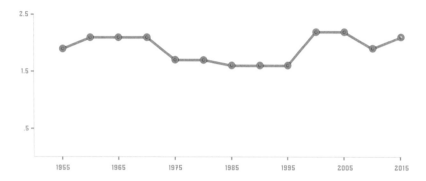

Charitable giving as % of GDP

Though our standard of living and amount of disposable income per person have risen a lot over the last 60 years, we still give about the same fraction of our resources to charity. That suggests there is significant room for more giving today—if a good case can be made to motivate donors.
In addition, new entrepreneurial tools make it possible for givers to accomplish more with a given amount of resources.

"When I graduated from business school I thought business was about making money, and philanthropy was about doing good. Now I think both can be used as methods for changing the world."
—Bill Ackman

We have people with radically different worldviews and backgrounds living cheek by jowl. This can either be a source of friction or a reservoir of alternative ideas on ways to improve life in our society. We can convert polarization into something positive—but only if we allow real autonomy and intellectual toleration.

We need competing local experiments where the ideas of different subcultures are tested in daily life so we can see which practices are actually good for human flourishing, and which are snake oil.

revolution." *Harvard Business Review* writer Paula Goldman quotes hedge-funder Bill Ackman's conclusion that "when I graduated from business school I thought business was about making money, and philanthropy was about doing good. Now I think both can be used as methods for changing the world."

And in all of this, philanthropic change generally comes with much less friction than politically driven change. As one social entrepreneur has put it, philanthropy relies on "the social dynamic of addition and multiplication," while government action often comes via "subtraction and division."

How to convert polarization into something positive

Division. One of the commonest refrains from present observers of American society is that we are fragmented and lack broad agreement on many issues. The positive pet phrase is that we are "diverse." The negative operating reality is that different segments of the population are often in sharp disagreement. To use the title of a recent book by Yuval Levin, we are *The Fractured Republic*.

Having lots of differences doesn't have to be a problem. There is actually deep strength in America's crazy-quilt of perspectives and interest groups, so long as:

1. we have clear-eyed means of assessing the outcomes of diverse behaviors, and then expanding the successes and shuttering the failures,
2. while meantime avoiding stepping on each other's toes (more on this in the next sub-section).

The key to making diversity a storehouse of strength instead of a disruptive sore is to let lots and lots of people invent their own solutions to problems within their own orbits, and eventually have them compete to see whose answers might have wider relevance and value to other elements of society. In some cases, what works in Utah may be very different from what works in New Jersey. In other instances, discoveries made in Utah may transfer perfectly well to lots of other places.

To find this out, we should encourage a social marketplace of micro-experiments in culture, social organization, family healing, moral teachings, economic incentives, and so forth. Rather than pretending we all share the same assumptions, want the same end results, have equally worthy goals, and are willing to put equal effort into realizing our goals, we need competing local laboratories—ranging from regional alliances to subcultures based on shared principles—where ideas can be developed in daily life so we can see which practices are actually good for human flourishing over an extended period, and which are snake oil.

Our country was set up on a "federalist" basis so that each state would have its own identity and many of its own peculiar ways of governing itself. Important social responsibilities like education, welfare payments, and transportation links were pushed even further down to county, city, or village governments. Our founders insisted on letting many flowers bloom, with confidence that people would migrate to the loveliest scents while leaving behind those that turned ugly.

Throughout our history there have been periodic attempts to reinforce the federalist quality of our nation. The 1980s, for instance, brought concerted efforts to shift some authority from officials in Washington to state and local governments. Nothing wrong with that, but what I am proposing here is much more thoroughgoing—lots of tasks should be shifted out of government altogether and handed off to the organs of civil society.

Because they will be locally tailored, these micro-experiments will vary in many crucial ways. Since they are philanthropic-voluntary, instead of government-mandatory, they will be gentler and more respectful of dissenting perspectives than even the smallest-scale government monopolies will ever be. "By empowering problem-solvers throughout American society, rather than hoping that Washington will get things right," argues Levin, we can "bring to public policy the kind of dispersed, incremental, bottom-up approach to progress that increasingly pervades every other part of American life." Micro-governance would also yield less feeling among Americans of being bossed or coerced, and a stronger sense of being involved in the community.

Real diversity—not balkanization, not enforced fashion
Note, however, that this will require true accommodation of diversity— not the fake diversity that is now promulgated by ideologues. Today's

Today's fake diversity hypes its openness to differences in things like skin color and sexual practice, but has scant tolerance for real dissent from fashionable views. Fake diversity kicks Boy Scouts out of public buildings, in cities that call themselves progressive.

fake diversity hypes its openness to differences in things like skin color and sexual practice, but has scant tolerance for real dissent from fashionable views. Boy Scouts of America principles don't match your views? Deny them use of public buildings! Catholic Charities wants to run its private adoption and foster-care service by placing children solely with married mother/father couples? Force them out of business in Boston, D.C., Illinois, and other places! Charitable job-training programs want to start hard-to-place workers at less than the minimum wage? Forbid it! Nonprofit hospitals decline to provide life-terminating procedures or "sex-reassignment" services among their offerings? Slap on financial penalties. Schools want to try single-sex classrooms? Sue them!

Fake tolerance "pays lip service to diversity but has narrow bandwidth for real differences," argue Kinnaman and Lyons. Fake tolerance insists that civil society must be a melting pot where intellectual and moral differences on contested issues are boiled down to a uniform conventional wisdom. "We all become the same. Anything *not* the same is, in the name of tolerance, skimmed off and thrown out. In this climate, those who dissent are evil and must be neutralized."

Kinnaman and Lyons, and other thinkers who are uncomfortable with this version of civil society that turns conscientious objectors into deviants, are calling for a true, "confident pluralism" that would substitute the potluck for the melting pot as a model for civil society. You bring fried chicken. I'll bring bean salad. Someone else will offer cupcakes. Visitors to the table can pick up what they want or need, and simply walk away from what they find unappealing.

Americans with viewpoints that do not cohere to current fashion must energetically defend their right to live and solve problems in their own ways. Kinnaman and Lyons, for instance, urge devoted Christians to shape themselves into "a principled counterculture for the common good." They should have no illusions that the elite establishment shares their convictions. But they should not hesitate to demand the liberty to find their own answers to modern life, unmolested so long as they remain within basic law. Yuval Levin urges that "rather than struggling for dominance of the increasingly weakened institutions of the mainstream culture" (which is what someone *must* do if he is contesting in politics), today's intellectual and moral dissenters should build "cohesive and attractive subcultures" that can prove out the viability of their social prescriptions.

These are prime tasks for civil society, philanthropy, and voluntary action. Down the road, successful subcultures can become models for wider reform and even political emulation. But in the meantime, people can build good lives according to their cherished principles, and keep evolved wisdom alive until our social fractures heal enough to allow its rediscovery by wider society.

This is not wishful thinking. Localized, non-uniform responses to human needs are what philanthropic entrepreneurs create all the time. The last two or three decades brought an explosion of private experiments seeking solutions to public problems, resulting in many triumphs like those I've been describing throughout this essay. The thousands of dispersed social reforms documented in *The Almanac of American Philanthropy* occurred in almost every sector of U.S. society, at a pace that accelerated during recent years.

Being truly respectful of differing intellectual perspectives, and devolving authority to groups of Americans so they can chip away at problems in their backyards in ways they think best, can do more than just make our communities function better. It can also help cure the popular unrest seen in the candidacies of Donald Trump and Bernie Sanders. The deepest and most understandable complaint of angry voters today, argues writer Andy Smarick, is their feeling of powerlessness, their sense that their concerns and perspectives are not represented in government, that their values are rarely enshrined in public policies. "The straightforward solution," he suggests, "is to give more people more power." And he adds a crucial coda: "The way to do that is decentralization."

Centerless self-rule

Soviet leader Nikita Khrushchev was convinced that the U.S. had a secret ministry of central planning hidden somewhere in Washington. An economy as big and successful as ours without someone in the middle giving orders? Inconceivable!

But the truth is, we are a country of centerless excellence. There is no one in charge of making sure that your local store doesn't run out of fresh milk. Yet it never does! In a culture where resources and authority are widely dispersed, people tend to their own needs very efficiently.

There is a great $50 word to describe this: Polyarchy. Polyarchy refers to a society in which there are many independent centers of power. (Contrast it to monarchy.) The United States has a notably polyarchic culture. And independent philanthropic giving is one big aspect of this. Go back to my earlier image portraying the millions of givers and charitable enterprises in our country as miniature legislatures that identify problems, develop fixes, and then act. It's a very, very dispersed style of social governance.

The constant downpour of individual charitable decisions leads to a much wider and multi-branched stream of national spending, and much better protection of non-mainline points of view, than any unitary government effort could provide. That's why Yale law professor Stephen Carter refers to philanthropy as "democracy in action."

The fact that most philanthropy takes place on a local level, usually out of the public eye, often on a private or even anonymous basis, means that it's very easy to overlook the force of this democracy in action. Most of us never see more than just a few small fragments of private giving at work. The result is that we grossly underestimate the problem-solving power of charitable action, and how valuable it is to our nation.

Moreover, you will regularly hear voluntary action criticized specifically for its polyarchic, decentralized nature. People complain that "philanthropy is not coordinated." Rules vary; there are holes; people go off in a hundred different directions. No one's in control!

Voluntary action is very different from the standardized uniformity of government programs. There's a problem with standardization, though: Human beings don't come in a standard model. And treating them as if they did will often have harmful effects.

The healthiest forms of society-building frequently vary over time and place—to match up better with particular people and specific conditions. The best solutions will often evolve in lots of little trial-and-error tests. Some efforts will fail, but the failures will be exposed and abandoned, and the successes will be copied. This kind of decentralized, results-based problem-solving is exactly where private philanthropy thrives.

Warren Buffett recently pointed out to journalist Nina Munk that when he's seeking investment home runs, "I'm looking for the easy pitches. I just wait for the one that's in my sweet spot. Philanthropy is just the opposite: You're dealing with problems that have resisted easy solutions." So in philanthropy he encourages his collaborators not to fear failure. "I've told them that unless they had failures, they *were* failures. It's the nature of philanthropy that you're going to fail." But when you do succeed through voluntary action's trial-and-error tests, you can often ride the wave for a very long way—because you have located the natural tides, and developed good human balance.

The potency of dispersed action has been brought into high relief by the computer revolution. As computerized problem-solving unfolded, it became clear that centralized control was ultimately inferior to lots and lots of small-scale, independent thinking. The story of the Internet is the accumulated power of millions of small actions. The lesson of the hacker culture is that one individual with a laptop can do astonishing things. The crowdsourcing of Wikipedia and Linux have blown away alternate solutions controlled from the top.

The deepest and most understandable complaint of angry voters today is their feeling of powerlessness, their sense that their concerns and perspectives are not represented in government, that their values are rarely enshrined in public policies. The solution is to decentralize power and let people govern themselves much more locally.

In addition to uncovering new ways of solving social problems, competing experiments in micro-governance would give citizens a deeper sense of being involved in the community, and less feeling of being bossed or coerced.

Many effective nonprofits like Goodwill (which provides billions of dollars of training and work experience every year to hard-to-employ Americans) are highly decentralized. The Goodwill network is made up of 163 autonomous regional affiliates, each with its own board, and funding, and methods.

Decentralized governance is obviously now a powerful trend in American business as well. Airbnbs are not uniform, as Holiday Inns or Marriotts are. Yet they are wildly popular with real people.

Many of our most productive nonprofits are extraordinarily decentralized. Goodwill is made up of 163 autonomous regional affiliates, each with its own board of directors, funding sources, and methods of operation. Habitat for Humanity is a network of 1,400 self-governing and self-funding local chapters. Fluttering over thousands of scientific breakthroughs produced by America's private research universities every year are highly scattered flocks of donor funders.

A recent article in *Education Week* reported that most education reforms of the last generation have turned out to be disappointingly feeble, but that bottom-up reforms have brought much more success than proposals dictated by education authorities. "The slower, decentralized approach…is not nearly as satisfying as advocating for huge sweeping changes," writes Mike McShane, but it has improved life for far more

students. "The broad, sweeping endeavors haven't lived up to the hype, and children have paid the price" every time a grand educational fad has been imposed from the top.

So the fact that philanthropy doesn't solve problems in a consistent way is nothing to criticize or apologize for. That civil society acts through a plethora of radically independent, small-scale, non-consistent entities should not be a concern. These are in fact some of the reasons that dispersed, non-governmental, voluntary problem-solving tends to be more efficacious.

The people's choice

The American people have already recognized the desirability of the approach I'm outlining here. Asked in a recent Heartland Monitor Poll what was most responsible for improvements in their local area over the past ten years, respondents picked "contributions by community organizations" over "government policies" by 2:1. Asked whether they would prefer that institutions stick to established paths or "try new ideas and solutions, even if the outcomes may be uncertain," the public favored experimentation by 71 percent to 20 percent.

In a 2016 survey for Independent Sector, 74 percent of voters said they would rather give their money to charities than to the federal government, and 78 percent said that they want government to engage more with charities to solve problems. When the Heartland respondents were asked where they think useful new ideas for addressing America's problems are most likely to come from, they picked "state and local institutions" over "national institutions" by 67 percent to 24 percent. Asked about their own region, fully 84 percent of Americans said the best solutions came from "programs by local volunteer and nonprofit organizations."

As gloomy as we are about the direction of the nation, Americans feel much more positive about trends in our local area. By 66 percent to 25 percent, people told the Heartland Monitor that their local region is headed in the right direction rather than the wrong direction.

Recent reporting echoes this data. *New York Times* columnist David Brooks traveled to some of the more economically stressed parts of the United States in the first half of 2016, then wrote up what he found: "The more time you spend in the hardest places, the more amazed you become. There's some movement arising that believes in the small moments of connection…. The social fabric is tearing across this country, but everywhere it seems healers are rising up to repair their small piece of it. They are going into hollow places and creating community, building intimate relationships that change lives one by one."

A similar essay in *The Atlantic* by James Fallows was based on scores of visits by small plane to unglamorous spots all across the country. He discovered myriad examples of "local resilience and adaptability" and "revival and reinvention" engineered by neighborhood organizers and givers. The closer you get to a community and its on-the-ground leaders, Fallows concluded, the more impressive America looks.

Even the Brookings Institution, which helped orchestrate much of our current concentration of authority in Washington, is now issuing reports rueing the fact that so much power, money, and elite expectation have become centered on the "executive juggernaut" in D.C. More "localism" is one Brookings proposal for curing widespread public disillusionment against the federal government. Clearly, both the American public and some open-minded elites are willing to try dramatically different ways of solving our cultural problems.

Dreaming up new paths; defending proven ones

So how do we find these missing solutions? "Imagination precedes fact," poet David Rowbotham reminds us. Contemporary America needs an imaginative burst of new charities, businesses, clubs, and schools capable of fixing social problems that vex us. We need original approaches and programs from existing institutions. We need fresh publishing, art, and historical research that stirs us and moves thinking beyond some very stale conventional wisdom.

We need social entrepreneurship that (to borrow a phrase from Kinnaman and Lyons) has a firm center but soft edges. That may be just the opposite of the way you like your eggs, but it is a good operating goal for reform-philanthropists: Establish a base camp on sturdy principle, and defend it against critics who would like to push you off. But never wall yourself in—keep your perimeter open so recruits can join up, have a sharp eye for new developments that may require you to shift tactics, and welcome all allies from whatever quarter.

Had the most to do with improving my area over the past ten years…

Business performance 32%

Community organizations 30%

Government policies 15%

Preferred approach to local challenges…

Try new ideas and solutions 71%

Rely on tried and tested ideas 20%

Better for community and country to give $1,000 to…

Charities 74%

Federal government 9%

Government should engage more with the charitable sector…

Agree 78%

Disagree 20%

New ideas and solutions are more likely to come from…

State and local institutions 67%

National institutions 24%

Volunteer and nonprofit organizations help my local area…

84%

Grassroots reporting matches what data and polling show: At the very local level, Americans are responding much more creatively to problems than our national government is.

You should expect the same openness in the camps of other social inventors. And if jealous or censorious government forces try to overrun you, fight back.

Be on guard to the fact that the ideological warriors who have destroyed our politics are also now lobbing shells into philanthropy and civil society. Several new kinds of attacks on private giving and givers are entering currency. Hostile reporters, activists, and politicians now paint images of "donor puppetmasters," complain that America is "privatizing the public good," conjure up conspiracies of "dark money," and claim that charitable dollars are actually "public" funds that should be subject to political steering.

Even venerable philanthropic triumphs like Teach For America and KIPP schools are under attack. TFA

2013 applicants to
Teach For America:
57,000

2016 applicants to
Teach For America:
37,000

is simultaneously criticized as elitist and as amateurish. It and KIPP are ripped for promulgating concepts of work, success, self-discipline, and excellence that radicals depict as "imposing cultural expectations" on the next generation. Ideological pressure is having effects: applications to TFA have tumbled 35 percent over the last three years.

Culture warriors have been even harsher on social entrepreneurs with a faith orientation. In advocacy groups, the media, and powerful corners of politics, there are now aggressive efforts to strip protections for speech and action based on religious conscience. There are efforts to push faith leaders and faith language out of the public square. There are proposals that religious organizations should be taxed. It's starkly new in the U.S. that such strains of argument would become so common.

People who value our remarkably productive civil society must make it a priority in coming years to protect the full participation of religious Americans. For in addition to threatening liberties at the heart of our country's founding, anti-religious attitudes and policies have the potential to undo much of our best social work. Practicing Christians are more than three times likelier than others to adopt or foster unwanted children. Catholic and other faith-based schools are a vital safety net for millions of poor students. The most effective programs for helping newly released convicts stay out of prison are ones run by religious volunteers. Much of our best work against homelessness has a religious motivation. The most efficient charities for aiding disaster victims and the poor overseas are faith-based. Anyone who cares about solving today's hardest social problems must defend the ability of faith entrepreneurs to operate freely.

This is not a political matter. Progressive activist and former Cornell University trustee Joseph Holland recently argued that energized religious activity would repair more of what ails America "than the grandiose theories of armchair secularists…than the perpetual pontifications of partisan politicians." He blew a clarion in his campus address:

What if students at colleges across America, perhaps starting with a chapter here at Cornell, resolved to give our nation a two hundred fiftieth birthday gift? A far-reaching foray to fix at long last America's racial breakdown, not decreed from the state houses but rising from the grassroots. A modern-day awakening that would inspire across the lines of race, ethnicity, and religion, to spiritually uplift the prosperous and materially uplift the poor, resulting in a refounding movement for our times.

There are many other places where America needs to keep minds and doors open to starkly new varieties of social reform. For instance, social scientist Charles Murray has recently proposed eliminating government social programs and instead providing a "universal basic income" of nearly $1,100 per month to every citizen. People in need of social services would be able to take their cash allotments to nonprofits or businesses to get help. Would this improve their chances of obtaining real, lasting solutions to their personal and family problems? That's worth thinking through and testing. Whether you view this as a dramatic policy proposal or just a thought experiment, there is much we can learn from giving real consideration to original ideas like this.

Civil society doesn't have magical powers. But it is composed of a vast variety of experience-tested operations of all complexions—secular and religious, material and moral, "conservative" or "liberal," national or local. Opportunities to match people seeking improvement to groups that have shown they can help should be grasped wherever possible. Even if our government remains gridlocked in the future, there are almost unlimited numbers of ways that America's free society can continue to be strengthened, as often as patriotic philanthropists decide to become involved.

Practical advice from the godfather

With this being a 25th anniversary of The Philanthropy Roundtable, it seems fitting as I close to invoke some cautionary wisdom from Irving Kristol. Kristol was an important American social thinker and a founder of the Roundtable. In a speech to the Council on Foundations in 1980 he encouraged philanthropists who want to strengthen our national fabric to begin in modest and practical ways, rather than overreach into large projects right away.

His first bit of advice: *Start small and be incremental.*

It really is possible to do good. Doing good isn't even hard. It's just doing a *lot* of good that is very hard. If your aims are modest, you

Progressives like Joseph Holland think moral inspiration and personal action will be much more effective than decrees from state houses at fixing societal weaknesses.

can accomplish an awful lot. When your aims become elevated beyond a reasonable level, you not only don't accomplish much, but you can cause a great deal of damage….

Foundations in this country have passed up enormous opportunities to do good, simply because…no one was satisfied with doing a little; everyone wanted to do a lot.

Second, Kristol urges: *Do what's achievable, and work with beneficiaries who are ready for a changed life.* Too many donors, he warns, insist that

"we want to help those who are really down at the bottom." But helping those at the bottom is not easy, whereas helping those who are moving up is feasible. It works.

Even before he helped found The Philanthropy Roundtable,
conservative thinker Irving Kristol offered useful advice
on how philanthropists can improve America.

If you suggest such a program you are accused of something
called "skimming the cream," namely, taking the most able,
the most intelligent, the most ambitious, and moving them up
while neglecting the rest. But that is the normal way in which
all groups move into the mainstream of American life…. You
begin by moving up those who can be moved up. Their brothers,
sisters, cousins, friends, see them moving up and begin to
foresee that it's possible. They begin to shape their lives and
their habits to follow them.

The notion that you go directly to the hard-core
unemployable…who are "hard-core" for a reason, is utopian….
The notion that you can…transform them overnight into willing
and eager students is childish…. It would be enormously
expensive, and in the end you would just be helping a few
individuals. The more sensible approach is to…help those

who wish to be helped, who can be helped, who are already
motivated…others will follow in their path.

Do what is doable…. You then get the kind of progress in
education, or in the economy, or what have you, which brings
everyone into the system.

Third, Kristol warns: *Don't get absorbed into the government blob.*

There is a tendency these days for everything to become
an adjunct to government, just as there is a tendency, when
foundations have a good idea, for government to take it and run
away with it…. So you end up with another government agency
doing, in its bureaucratic way, what neighbors were doing in a very
pleasant and humane way….

To the degree that our society becomes more centralized, to the
degree that government becomes more intrusive in all the affairs of
our lives…foundations are going to be assimilated into government.

There are many ways to elevate America

I would extend Irving Kristol's advice with one more practical
warning: When you are deciding where you want to apply yourself as a
philanthropy-patriot, don't overlook what C. Z. Nnaemeka has referred
to as the "unexotic" needy. Yes, Kenyans without clean water, heroin
addicts, high-school dropouts, AIDS victims, homeless children—
these people need charitable help. But their needs are already much
proclaimed. There are other less exotic needy persons being overlooked
and underserved. Older people let go from jobs. Veterans languishing
in our dysfunctional disability system. Single mothers in rural areas. It's
important that donors not move as a trendy pack. Methodically seek out
citizens in your universe who need help and aren't receiving it.

And one last thing for public-spirited philanthropists to bear in mind:
Those of you whose philanthropic passions are unrelated to deep social
reform shouldn't feel like there is less purpose in what you do. Don't
imagine that only philanthropists who support think tanks, heal wounded
soldiers, restore the Lincoln Memorial, or fight Zika are serving the
nation. There are thousands of ways to elevate America.

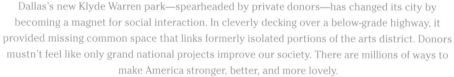

Dallas's new Klyde Warren park—spearheaded by private donors—has changed its city by becoming a magnet for social interaction. In cleverly decking over a below-grade highway, it provided missing common space that links formerly isolated portions of the arts district. Donors mustn't feel like only grand national projects improve our society. There are millions of ways to make America stronger, better, and more lovely.

It isn't just grand national projects that improve our society. Simple charitable comforts, direct personal assistance, art that inspires, soothing parks, spiritual faith that brings healing, underwriting for local pillar institutions—these traditional charitable priorities are vital contributions to making our nation good. Money spent effectively on kindness, truth, beauty, and moral uplift can be every bit as therapeutic for individuals—and for a country—as money spent on medical care and job training and schooling.

Donors and volunteers can be proud of any well-aimed contributions that make people happier and healthier, and strengthen our communal life. So don't feel limited by rigid boundaries when pursuing social improvement and culture change.

The key is just to take a part. To contribute directly. To act—rather than waiting for some distant, divided, impersonal agency to solve our problems for us. ⌃

— A CASE STUDY —

Changing Society through Civil Action

America's Second Great Awakening

The religious revival that swept America in the years before our Revolution—known as the Great Awakening—deepened our belief in human sovereignty and equality before God, and was thereby a crucial factor, historians agree, in fueling our struggle for independence.

A full generation later there followed a Second Great Awakening. It was even more influential in forming our national character and changing the direction of our society. While the first awakening produced political change, the second awakening yielded social reform—shifting American culture in ways both broad and deep.

The bloom was off the rose of politics for Americans as the Second Great Awakening began at the end of the 1700s and accelerated in the early decades of the 1800s. This was when the Articles of Confederation imploded, partisan hatreds broke out for the first time, the nation became embroiled again in war, and passionate Jacksonian populism smashed all sorts of national customs and forms. The social changes of the day were drastic, and politics was chaotic. "No period" of U.S. history "was

more concerned with ideological issues than the age of Jackson," notes historian Bertram Wyatt-Brown. This produced not only bitter electoral contention but also struggles over the staffing of government, spurts of corruption, and periodic violence in our streets and town squares. Many Americans felt unsettled and uneasy.

Not only our politics but our culture seemed debased. Per capita alcohol use was three to four times current levels. (See Temperance case study.) Public spaces were often slimy with tobacco spit. Popular pastimes included dogfights, cockfights, rats-versus-dog battles, and bull-baiting. A fighting style called "gouging" was a problem during these decades. Street brawlers grew their fingernails long to make it easier to pop the eyeball out of an opponent's head; some filed their teeth to assist in biting off appendages during frequent imbroglios.

Disgust with ugly politics and culture didn't drive solid citizens into retreat, though. To the contrary, philanthropists—and especially the surging ranks of reborn evangelical Christians—decided that they had a duty to help create a better and more orderly nation. And this was history's first religious revival that aimed to simultaneously serve God and soften Caesar. Believers were urged to be active on two distinct fronts: soul-saving *and* good citizenship; personal character *and* neighborhood decency; abstaining from evil *and* rooting out evils in society; salvation *and* reform; religion *and* humanitarianism; individual regeneration *and* cultural improvement. It was not an otherworldly religion that swept America in the first half of the nineteenth century. Leaders like Charles Finney argued that the Gospel had been given to us by God not only to rescue souls but to clean up our collective life.

Change was happening in Britain at the same time. English philanthropist and politician William Wilberforce, who led his nation's crusade to abolish the slave trade, emblemized the evangelical enthusiasm for spreading religious and moral truths to all people, regardless of station, while also emphasizing the vital need for "a reformation of manners" in collective life. But the evangelical wave swept further into the countryside in America than it did in Britain, creating a surge of social energy that left deep marks on secular life.

Protestant church membership in the U.S. grew twice as fast as population over the multidecade course of the Second Great Awakening. In areas where the revival fires burned brightest, like upstate New York, religious activity was rampant. Even more impressive than the packed church pews, remarked newspapers like the *Rochester Observer,* was the "spirit of zeal and boldness" and "increased energy infused into Christian character and exertion."

The 1853 report of a traveler from Sweden named Fredrika Bremer gives a flavor of the passion in evidence at revival peaks. She describes an immense crowd of mingled white and black Americans at a nighttime Georgia camp meeting. Eight large altars had been built in a forest. Scores of campfires roared, with rings of burbling people gathered around each. She records wails from the penitent as a lightning storm approaches, and describes joyful singing by thousands of believers. It was, she writes, a night "never to be forgotten."

Mass inner transformation connected to outward action
One of the remarkable things about the Second Great Awakening is how democratic it was. It was sparked

Jacksonian America was an often cruel society. Depicted here is one of the many bloody spectacles staged at Kit Burns's Sportsmen's Hall in New York City. Classes high and low came to gamble on terriers set against 100 rats, no-holds-barred human fights, bear-baiting, death matches between dogs, even battles between barehanded men and pit bulls.

Powerful moral reform ended slavery, universalized literacy, and cemented what we now think of as the classic American virtues.

One of the thousands of outdoor revival meetings that burst forth across America during the first half of the nineteenth century. Storytelling, teaching, and preaching inspired religious conversions that caused church membership to grow twice as fast as our population over a multi-decade period.

and initially peopled by Methodist, Baptist, and Presbyterian farmers, artisans, and laborers. Only after small-town residents and frontier families had built it into a mighty force did it eventually become a gravitational influence on wealthier classes. The theology of the awakening centered around the equal value and wide opportunity enjoyed by every person. It rejected all conceptions of an anointed elect, an aristocratic church, or an elitist view of the good life.

One of the leaders who imbued the movement with this accessible spirit was Charles Finney. An upstate New York attorney prior to his conversion, he brought a democratic spirit and host of effective courtroom techniques to his second career of lifting up Americans from the pulpit. The effect was powerful.

Finney's preaching was not only exciting and impassioned, but direct, logical, and sincere. He urged all pastors to speak in simple cogent sentences and clear colloquial language. He always used the first-person "you," not some fuzzy third-person reference. His precise, logical arguments delivered with energy, verve, and informal wit resembled a great "lawyer arguing to a jury," in the

words of one impressed observer. Businessmen, practical artisans, and students loved his messages.

The first aim of his frank, dramatic preaching was to convince the listener to take the Christian message to heart and change his or her own life in intimate, lasting ways. His immediate second priority was to build a sense of what he called "present obligation" among his listeners. He wanted the farmers and merchants, mechanics and mothers in his audience to recognize their responsibilities to others, and enter into service of their fellow man. This marriage of inner personal change to humanitarian action was the great contribution of evangelical activists during this era.

In a series of camp meetings conducted from 1825 to 1835, Finney drew vast crowds, particularly in central and western New York. To build on the following he stirred up in small towns, fast-growing new cities, and frontier regions, philanthropists like Arthur Tappan, William Dodge, Anson Phelps, and Jonas Platt provided funding to bring his revival message to big Eastern cities including Manhattan. They rented churches for him, hired assistants, provided publicity, and offered funds to eliminate the pew fees that made it hard for people of modest income to attend services in major sanctuaries.

"No more impressive revival has occurred in American history," writes historian Whitney Cross in assessing Finney's work. Charles Finney was "one of those rare individuals who of their own unaided force may on occasion significantly transform the destinies of masses of people."

Finney had lots of company in wedding revivalism to social reform. His fellow preacher and reformer Lyman Beecher spent much of his career working to convince fellow Americans that Christianity was more about what they should *do* than about what they could think. The linking of religious belief to constructive social behavior was such a strong emphasis that by the end of the Second Great Awakening it had become a truism even of Senate speeches. "I believe man can be elevated; man can become… more God-like in his character, and capable of governing himself. Let us go on elevating our people, perfecting our institutions," urged Senator Andrew Johnson in 1858.

Bringing morality to politics

The new reforming religion that surged across America in the first half of the nineteenth century had a fascinating relationship to politics. As the Second Great Awakening arrived, many secular reformers were ready for help from religious leaders. They were finding it difficult to improve our tumultuous country through policy alone.

Benjamin Rush is a perfect example. A physician and signer of the Declaration of Independence, he was a reform philanthropist who did vast good in areas like improved medical care, humane treatment of the insane, prison reform, and education of the poor and neglected. He was also one of the first prominent Americans to warn that heavy drinking was damaging our society and that alcohol consumption patterns needed to change. He wrote a book on the physiological and social damage done by bingeing, and worked with other humanitarians like Pennsylvania philanthropist Anthony Benezet to try to make headway against this problem. Rush eventually concluded that churches were best positioned to bring lasting reductions in drinking, writing that,

from the influence of the Quakers and Methodists in checking this evil, I am disposed to believe that the

Charles Finney was an attorney turned pastor who stirred up enormous religious enthusiasm during the Second Great Awakening. He was a logical preacher who argued like a great lawyer speaking to a jury. His marriage of inner personal change to humanitarian action was characteristic of evangelical activists during this era.

These are to CERTIFY that William Warren was duly elected a MEMBER of the

INDEPENDENT BENEVOLENT SOCIETY OF PHILADELPHIA

An explosion of new benevolent groups went to work against poverty, family breakdown, ignorance, and other social problems. This ecosystem of volunteer societies, known as the Benevolent Empire, received total annual donations rivaling the size of the entire federal budget of the day.

business must be effected finally by religion alone. Human reason has been employed in vain…. We have nothing to hope from the influence of *law* in making men wise and sober.

As the Second Great Awakening was unfolding, American politics, like much of the rest of the country, was in the midst of turmoil and far-reaching change. Many members of the possessing classes were turning away from the Federalists in frustration. A raw new populist streak was unfolding across public life, including in the presidency of Andrew Jackson and the party machines that took over many major cities. Mass political parties were being born for the first time in human history. Dramatically different strategies for winning office and governing were taking root, and Americans were having to learn whole new ways of thinking about political action.

Evangelical Christians were most concerned with individual behavior and reinforcing the moral rules that yield success in both personal life and public affairs. Many Christian reformers were wary of political contamination of religious causes, and political corruption of well-meant reforms. But they did not turn their backs on the new politics. They knew that the political arena was one of the necessary forums where personal behavior and community morals had to be discussed and regulated. Though their consciences often tempted them to opt out of politics, the vast majority resisted and instead tried to fashion principled codes of public action that would sometimes include political activity.

Yet they were clear on which form of activity was the higher and subsumed the other. Instead of arguing that "religion has a legitimate role in politics," as is often said today, Charles Finney put the horse before the cart, saying that "politics are a part of religion in such a country as this." Philanthropist and leading New York financier Thomas Eddy insisted that people saying "we take no interest in politics" were really saying "we take no interest in human progress." They were also, he warned, abandoning the freedoms of religious conscience and practice that were so hard-won by America's founders. Other leaders called an anti-political temper "un-Christian," castigated "the piety that is too ethereal for the duties of citizenship," and urged that "Christians must do their duty to the country as part of their duty to God." Editor and Methodist pastor James Watson suggested that true religion "sanctifies the citizen and sends him to the ballot-box to… bless his fellow man."

Historian Richard Carwardine concludes that this insistence on bringing religious conscience to the creation of public policy shaped our politics "every bit as much as appeals to natural law and natural rights had molded the politics of the Revolutionary era." The Second Great Awakening pushed the political emphasis away from naked interests and the idea that "to the victor belongs the spoils," which dominated the early 1800s, toward a more morally principled approach.

This shift is nicely illustrated in one concrete bit of evidence. The very first time that Lewis Tappan—the leading reform-philanthropist of the Second Great Awakening—ever saw a win by the candidate he supported for President was in 1864. Abraham Lincoln became the greatest moralist ever elected to our top political office just as the social reforms spurred by the Awakening reached a high-water mark.

Grassroots activism

Much more than politics, though, civil society was the place where leaders and funders of the Second Great Awakening put their energy and resources. They created hundreds of charities, associations, and action groups to fan out across the country and make conditions healthier, happier, and more wholesome. The products of this grassroots effort included orphanages, old-age homes, houses for delinquent children, hospitals, residences and job-training programs for former prostitutes, new or expanded churches, shelters for the poor, legal defense for Native Americans facing removal from their lands, anti-alcohol self-help groups, Sunday schools, seminaries, new colleges, schools catering to girls and blacks and Native Americans, advocacy for the rights of wives whose husbands had abandoned them, clubs that discouraged profanity among children, and groups that pushed businesses to close on Sunday and let their workers rest and worship with their families. These creations were crucial in bringing cohesion, order, decency, fairness, and stability to jam-packed cities and rough frontiers where many virtues had leaked away.

Awakened citizens gave money and raised it from their friends, and they volunteered their time and labor in vast quantities. "Members were not to attempt to do good merely by pecuniary contributions, but especially by personal exertions and labors. Every member of the Society was to be 'a working man,'" wrote the organizer of one charity created to teach children.

This approach characterized the Second Great Awakening's style of Protestantism—which emphasized "personal exertions" and the need to work for the salvation and success of others. One important sociological benefit of this was that it got millions of middle-class businessmen and housewives and college students into direct contact with the poor, slaves, drunkards,

From Andrew Jackson's election in 1828 to Abraham Lincoln's Presidency one full generation later, American behaviors, attitudes, manners, religious practices, and political ideas were dramatically reshaped. The leadership of persons of faith, forward-looking businessmen, and middle-class donors and volunteers was crucial in making this happen.

Reformers didn't possess extraordinary wisdom; they just experimented with solutions to social problems and then focused on those that worked best.

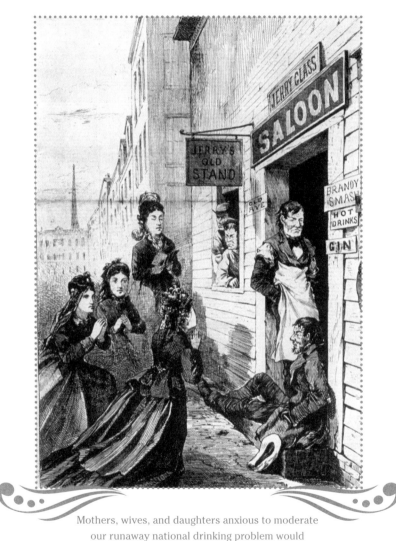

Mothers, wives, and daughters anxious to moderate our runaway national drinking problem would sometimes stage prayer vigils at saloons, reducing alcohol consumption through encouragement, shame, and personal appeals.

lonely seamen, abandoned widows, and disenfranchised minorities. The helpers thus developed real understanding and expertise in what was going on in our tenements and docks and servants' quarters.

This led the evangelical activists to try a vast range of new palliatives—visiting nurses, milk stations for children, hostels to protect new arrivals from the country from urban corruptions, you name it. Many individuals and groups found themselves offering multiple kinds of help at the same time: Women visiting elderly people in need of company also brought food. At church services in poor neighborhoods, clothing, coal, bread, and jobs were distributed along with Bibles and tracts. Missionaries who moved into slums to proselytize also ended up teaching the ABCs to young and old neighbors. Reformers developed a vast arsenal of weapons for battling irreligion, ignorance, and want. "Early nineteenth-century evangelicals did not possess extraordinary vision or wisdom; they merely experimented with various solutions to the problems they saw and then focused their energies on those that seemed to work best," reports historian Anne Boylan.

Many talented organizers and leaders rose to the top of the reform groups working to clean up our society: people like the gifted polemicist Theodore Weld, the poet John Greenleaf Whittier, and journalist-provocateur William Lloyd Garrison. Though the mores of their era kept most out of the limelight, many top charitable efforts depended heavily on impressive women as the foot soldiers and line officers of their battalions, and nearly all of the eventual leaders of the later suffrage and women's rights movements were alumni of these evangelical reform groups.

The burst of cooperative and transformative energy that poured out in communities all across our land also produced larger alliances that either coordinated the local groups or operated as national or international charities in their own right. Look beneath their sometimes ornate nineteenth-century titles and you will get a sense of the breathtaking ambition of these associations, which quickly numbered in the thousands: the Society for Bettering the Condition of the Poor, Provident Society for Employing the Poor, Society for the Promotion of Industry Among the Poor, American Education Society, Society for Establishment and Support of Charity Schools, American Temperance Society, Sons and Daughters of Temperance, American Bible Society, American Tract Society, Prison Discipline Society, Orphan Asylum Society, American Female Guardian Society, American Seamen's Friend Society, American Home Missionary Society, Board of Commissioners for Foreign Missions, American Sunday School Union, American Anti-Slavery Society.

Collectively, this remarkable ecosystem of volunteer societies became known as the Benevolent Empire. And empire is not too strong a word. By 1834, when the voluntary wave was still in its early days, the total annual income donated to the major Benevolent Empire groups rivaled the size of the entire federal budget of that year. Most of the charities had broad bases and were sustained by hundreds of thousands of modest donations from contributors all across small-town America. "The real dependence of the movement," reports Wyatt-Brown, "was upon the middle-class farmers and townsmen near the Erie Canal and along the rivers of New England."

Puritan entrepreneurs

Wealthy philanthropists also played important roles. Ground Zero for the interlocking reform groups was Nassau Street in lower Manhattan—where many of the evangelical charities were headquartered. Nassau Street begins directly in front of today's New York Stock Exchange. Then as now, the merchants and financiers whose places of business packed that region included many nationally important philanthropists. Generous givers among the lower-Manhattan capitalists, plus other major donors like Stephen Van Rensselaer, Gerrit Smith, Theodore Frelinghuysen, Elias Boudinot, William Jay, Richard Varick, James Milnor, John Pintard, and Thomas Eddy, were important seed funders for many charitable efforts.

Foremost among the spark-plug philanthropists supporting the Benevolent Empire were the Tappans. Their large family included two prosperous and philanthropic brothers in Boston, another brother who became a U.S. Senator, plus additional siblings. But it was New York City merchants Arthur and Lewis who became the most famous of the Tappans. I suggest that from the Wrights to the Kennedys to the Kochs, no other pair of brothers

Families would descend on neighborhoods to give the poor Bibles, tracts, food, and clothing. Vast volunteer efforts connected citizens across divides of wealth, ethnicity, faith, and region.

even came close to having as big a transformative effect on America as these two philanthrocapitalists.

Arthur and Lewis Tappan grew up in a very pious home in small-town New England. Their village of Northampton, Massachusetts, "was neither rich and sophisticated, nor backward and poor," records one chronicler. Their modestly successful family likewise adopted the classic middle-American perspective and avoided being either haughty or submissive.

Mrs. Tappan was a grandniece of Benjamin Franklin, but the family "put on no airs, envied no one's superior status, and did not snub those below them," according to Wyatt-Brown.

Their community was stitched together by the threads of numerous voluntary associations of the sort that Tocqueville marveled over during his American tours at the height of our Second Great Awakening. For instance,

From the Wrights
to the Kennedys to the Kochs,
no other pair of brothers
came close to having as big a
transformative effect on America
as these two philanthro-capitalists.

The Second Great Awakening began in the towns and small cities of upstate New York and western New England, spreading along the Erie Canal and various river valleys into the frontier communities of our Midwest. Later, it arrived in our major cities.

Northampton's solid citizens would gather before the fireplace of the town inn once every month and convene their Society for Detecting Thieves and Robbers and Bringing Them to Punishment. Their Hampton Musical Society met in the same building—but weekly rather than monthly, putting the lie to the idea that Puritans were all grim duty and no melodious fun.

There's no doubting the Tappans were Puritans. In her youth, Mrs. Tappan attended revivals with George Whitefield and other leading preachers of the original Great Awakening. And the home where she and Mr. Tappan reared their flock for a period of years was the former residence of fire-and-brimstone preacher Jonathan Edwards. Many notes and tones of America's previous spiritual crescendo echoed around Arthur and Lewis as they grew to adulthood.

The boys had an uncle David who was a professor at Harvard. In a letter where he mourned the political disruptions and personal "infidelity, impiety, and vice" of the early 1800s, Dr. David Tappan recommended the writings of the British philanthropist and politician William Wilberforce. The ideas and example of Wilberforce were a perfect guide, he suggested, to "ardent piety and patriotism and philanthropy."

In his marriage, Arthur tapped into another public-spirited American family with a tradition of service. His bride grew up in the New York City home of Alexander Hamilton. Her father had been one of Hamilton's closest friends during the Revolution, so when both of her parents died by the time she was two, Hamilton stepped in as surrogate father and raised her like one of his own offspring.

As young men, both Arthur and Lewis pitched in on a variety of charitable causes. In his early working years Lewis became secretary of the local benevolent society, served as a church treasurer, helped edit a magazine called the *Christian Register*, and volunteered as a counselor with a temperance group. He donated money, and raised it from others, to support the Deaf and Dumb Asylum, the Hospital for the Sick, the Asylum for the Insane, and the Asylum for Indigent Boys. He supported the American Bible Society, and helped start the Boston Provident Institution—one of the very first banks created to make it easier for the poor to accumulate wealth.

After the textile business Lewis had built to success became overextended and went bankrupt, he went to work in Arthur's silk-selling firm as a partner. The two labored hand-in-glove for much of the rest of their lives. When he saw up close the life Arthur had created as a Christian businessman and philanthropist in Manhattan, Lewis was deeply impressed. His brother was already making a remarkably wide array of deep charitable gifts. He built libraries where young apprentices newly relocated from countryside to city could go to educate themselves and socialize off the corrupting streets. He was a director of the Seaman's Friend Society that offered aid and companionship to elderly sailors. He supported many churches in lower Manhattan. Looking over his brother's profoundly ambitious experiment in Christian living, Lewis marveled that "this is enjoying riches in a high degree…in the good he achieves while living."

The power of a few good men
Though they labored in close parallel for decades, and agreed on nearly all matters of principle and practice, Arthur and Lewis Tappan had very different personalities, and achieved their good works in quite different fashions. Arthur was taciturn, sensitive, and a bit forbidding. He kept no guest chairs in his small office because he believed they only encouraged visitors to tarry, distracting him from getting things done.

Lewis was much more social, indeed a tireless extrovert, and a powerful public speaker. He "performed the muscular work" that allowed both the brothers' business ventures and the scores of philanthropic projects they jointly supported to thrive. He was a master strategist and natural leader, and showed repeated brilliance at capitalizing on current events, turning them into object lessons for the American public—as in the case of the *Amistad* trial that he orchestrated into a turning point on national opinion toward slavery. (See the abolition case study.)

Yet even at the peak of his fame, Lewis always made time to join small prayer meetings, visit the sick, and hand out Bibles in the sterile countinghouses lining Wall Street or the dank taverns that sprouted like mushrooms along the East River wharves. There were occasions where he and several compatriots charged into grim brothels "to

Brothers Lewis (top) and Arthur (bottom) Tappan were pioneering businessmen, and even more remarkable as philanthropic organizers of both personal transformation and social change. They pioneered a "comprehensive" style of civic action that left deep imprints on America in numerous sectors.

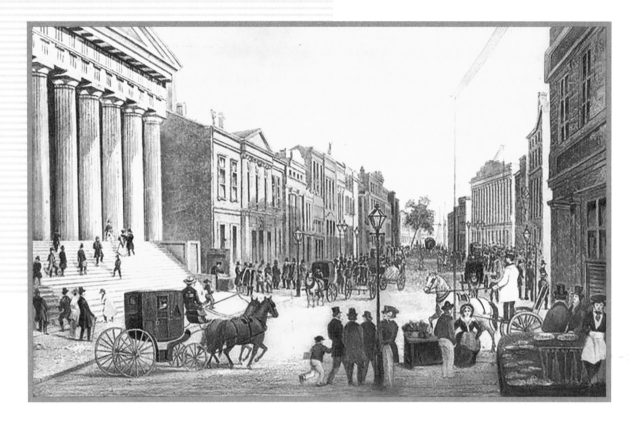

In 1846, when this scene at the corner of Wall Street and Broad was captured, the financial district of lower Manhattan was (like today) home turf for many nationally influential philanthropists. Important charities of the "Benevolent Empire" were headquartered nearby along Nassau Street.

pluck fallen women from roaring lions who seek to devour them," placing their rescues in homes run by clergy that supplied food and clothing, Bible studies, and occupational training to allow the women to support themselves in respectable employment.

For most of their lives, Arthur was much wealthier than Lewis, and a far heavier donor. (But then, he was a heavier donor than perhaps anyone else in his half

century.) Arthur was abstemious and frugal, spending almost nothing on himself, and modestly on his family. He viewed his money as a resource entrusted to him by Providence, to be used accountably to improve life on earth and lift men's eyes to higher goals. In typical seasons he gave away the lion's share of his yearly income.

Arthur Tappan had a razor-sharp philanthropic vision and the courage

to put down large sums for difficult or unpopular work. He was one of the first American philanthropists to act on a "comprehensive" scale—founding organizations where he found them wanting, sticking with recipient groups through thick and thin over decades, making huge investments in particular charities as they hit a crossroads, pursuing long-term goals.

Almost without exception, Arthur left speaking and writing to others. He made his contributions by volunteering his managerial expertise behind the scenes, soliciting fellow members of his New York City merchant class to pitch in for charitable causes, and making heavy gifts of his own (even when his business and income were tottering). Arthur Tappan's main means of expressing himself, as one biographer put it, was "the metallic eloquence of his money."

And that was a huge contribution. "Our great benevolent system owes its expansion and power to his influence," observed one contemporary. "His example inspired the merchants of New York… leading them to give hundreds and thousands where before they gave tens and fifteens."

Because Arthur committed very little to print, never made a public address, and often gave in secret, it is hard to be concrete in totaling his donations. But by the 1820s he was known as the most generous donor in New York City. Lewis, his business and charitable partner, estimated that Arthur gave away roughly $50,000 every year for decades. John Pintard, a formidable businessman and Christian philanthropist in his own right, marveled in 1830 that "he is truly a wonderful benefactor and…his benefactions may amount in a few years to half a million…. I wish we had more Arthur Tappans."

His renown was international. After he was chosen to head the American Anti-Slavery Society (to which he was the lead donor), British philanthropists sent the society a note. "Your officers, with that indefatigably devoted, great and good man, Arthur Tappan as your president," they wrote, "give assurance that you must conquer."

Purifying business and enriching the nation

Along with painter, inventor, and Morse-code developer Samuel Morse, Arthur founded the *New York Journal of Commerce* in 1827. He showed additional inventiveness here. The newspaper, for instance, operated two fast ocean-going schooners that intercepted ships

returning to New York so that overseas business and political news collected from the crew could be published in the *Journal* a day or two before everyone else got it.

Arthur's deepest motivation for starting another newspaper was his frustration that there was no available business publication free of "immoral advertisements" for liquor, tobacco, Sunday theater entertainments, and such. Arthur lost $30,000 in the first few years of running the paper, yet continued to turn down easy ad money from sources he considered unwholesome. Eventually, his journal grew into one of the era's leading financial and political papers, demonstrating that righteous commerce was not an unpractical dream. (An offshoot is still published today, 190 years later.)

Both Tappan brothers were watchdog capitalists throughout their lives. After retiring, Lewis wrote a book titled *Is it Right to be Rich?* It was an indictment of the quick-money schemes and materialism that erupted after our Civil War.

Arthur brought his benevolence right into his workplace. He tried to assist and shelter his young apprentices and clerks—steering them to respectable rooming houses and active churches, setting

Arthur Tappan founded the *New York Journal of Commerce*, pictured above. He paid a heavy financial price for turning down advertisements he considered degrading or immoral, but used innovations to build the paper into an economic and political force.

Arthur Tappan had a razor-sharp philanthropic vision, and the courage to put down large sums for difficult or unpopular work.

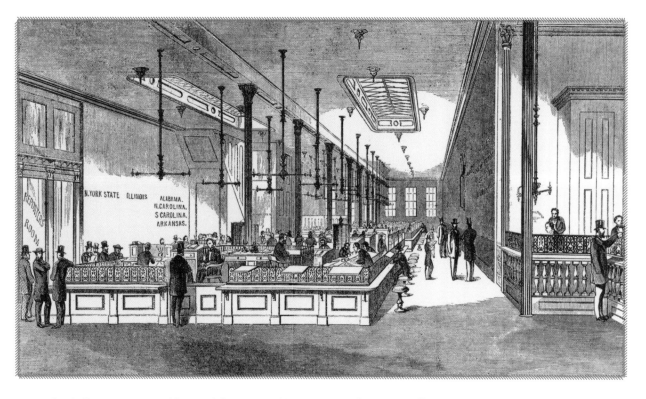

Lewis Tappan came up with a crucial commercial innovation: credit reporting. Drawing on connections made in his charitable work, he recruited a network of correspondents to file character reports on merchants all across the country, so their qualifications for credit could be assessed. His "Mercantile Agency"—whose New York City headquarters is depicted here—eventually grew into Dun and Bradstreet.

brothers had seen firsthand that borrowing money, buying goods on credit, and accumulating debt could tempt people to lie, exploit others, or walk away from responsibilities. A store owner from St. Louis or New Orleans could come to New York, fill a boat with wholesale goods purchased on credit, then never be seen again. There were few mechanisms for discouraging this.

Disquiet over the ways that easy money could warp men eventually led the Tappans into a world-changing business venture. Lewis launched an entirely new industry—credit reporting—that married their dual interests in personal character and private enterprise. His Mercantile Agency recruited correspondents in cities and towns all across the country—700 of them by 1846—to compile confidential reports on the reliability, honesty, and stability of merchants in their area. Arthur joined him in expanding this venture.

As information sources, Lewis drew heavily on people of high ethics he knew through his philanthropic work in abolition, Sunday schooling, temperance, and other causes. He particularly favored local pastors and small-town lawyers as correspondents. Abraham Lincoln became one of

aside a room in the company headquarters for prayer and Bible study, and maintaining contact with the small-town parents who entrusted their sons to him to be trained. He was generous in setting up his successful employees in independent careers, and eventually many of his biggest business competitors were former associates whom he had launched into trade with his own money.

Arthur and Lewis became known as honest and fair dealers. They set prices low, depending on heavy volume for their profits. They both hated loans and usurious credit—due to Biblical injunctions, and because they believed that borrowing money often corrupted the good habits and character of merchants. As much as possible they did business in cash, or used quickly redeemed promissory notes at low or no interest.

Commerce in the Tappans' day was often conducted on the honor system. With the country growing rapidly and morals changing, this was becoming less tenable. The his agency's Midwestern reporters; storekeeper Ulysses Grant another. (Grover Cleveland and William McKinley also filed reports for a time, making Tappan's firm perhaps the only one in U.S. history to have employed four future Presidents while they were young men.)

The Mercantile Agency built, and constantly updated, an archive with brief dossiers on the economic record, personal character, and trustworthiness of thousands of traders. Merchants considering extending credit to a provincial buyer would ask the agency for a report on their potential partner. By rewarding honest merchants and punishing those who neglected responsibilities, Tappan's commercial creation thus filled a moral gap. As Lewis himself put it, this mechanism "checks knavery, and purifies the mercantile air."

In the words of Lewis's biographer Bertram Wyatt-Brown,

His Agency was answering a specific need that those institutions which he so much appreciated himself—the church, the family, and the small-town community— were no longer capable of supplying. At one time, the local minister, a relative, or a neighbor could furnish the appraisal of an applicant that a creditor needed. By the 1840s, the country had grown too large and too populated and its people were too mobile for the old sources of information to function efficiently.

Subscribers soon found the service indispensable, and business mushroomed. The Tappan company eventually evolved into today's Dun & Bradstreet.

Credit reporting put a rational basis beneath the distribution of capital (which is the lifeblood of commerce). By reducing loan defaults, it allowed lenders to lower interest rates, fueling American expansion. In reducing the uncertainties of business transactions, credit reporting "played a vital role in building the twentieth-century American economic system," concludes Wyatt-Brown, who compares it to the telegraph, the railroad, and the free press in setting the stage for modern prosperity.

This Tappan innovation was thus able to simultaneously clean up American business, supercharge the economy, and create new incentives for ethical behavior—the kind of trifecta every reformer dreams of. ⏫

The Mercantile Agencies.
They Have Grown Indispensable to Business.

WITHOUT the mercantile agency the modern wholesale merchant would not know how to do business. It is true the wholesale merchant's grandfather did very nicely without the mercantile agency, but then they were such be kept. It was seen that one man giving his entire time to the work of looking after the standing of dealers seeking credit could accomplish more with greater economy and thoroughness than was possible for any small number of merchants to do. This was what led to the establishment of the first mercantile agency under the name of Lewis Tappan & Co.

The Tappans' credit reports were a seminal creation—simultaneously establishing new incentives for moral behavior by individuals, supercharging the U.S. economy, and cleaning up unethical business practices. Both as social and commercial entrepreneurs, the brothers were mold-breakers.

Disgust with ugly politics and culture didn't drive solid citizens into retreat. It instead drove them to create a remarkable ecosystem of charitable organizations that transformed America.

— A CASE STUDY —

Changing Society through Civil Action

Sunday Schools

On their own, children grow, play, learn, and eventually reach adulthood. They become educated, however, only if somebody provides that for them. In the first half of the nineteenth century, only about 50 percent of American children were given formal schooling.

Many of the others missed school because they were sent out to work. Trudging off to jobs or farm work six days a week, they had no opportunity to pick up reading, writing, and arithmetic. So at an accelerating pace from the early 1800s on, a large group of volunteers and donors went to work to compensate for that—by offering free literacy lessons (and much more) on the one day when almost everyone had free time: Sunday.

The founders of Sunday schools were especially concerned about poor and working-class children, newly arrived immigrants, and disadvantaged minorities, and began their efforts there. They first taught youngsters the alphabet, then how to read and write, and sometimes arithmetic. They trained children in valuable techniques of memorization. They used the Bible as a main text, and transmitted religious knowledge and lots of character training while providing the tools of communication.

These schools tapped into deep hungers in the U.S. population, and became wildly popular. Many poor children picked up more of their literacy, and their moral compass, at Sunday school than they did in our uneven, inadequate, and often nonexistent public schools. Adult Sunday schools were also formed so "mechanics" and other laboring men could be instructed outside of working hours. Organizers placed schools in factories, homes, shops, and other public buildings in addition to churches, to make sure they reached those in need. "As an agency of cultural transmission," concludes the leading historian on this topic, the Sunday school run by volunteers "rivaled in importance the nineteenth-century public school" created by government.

A focus on the least

"In the United States of America, the progress of Sunday schools has been truly astonishing," observed an 1820 report from Britain. "Schools are formed in almost every considerable town and village. They have extended to the…Indian tribes, and have spread particularly among the blacks."

Though black children and adults were blocked from many other forms of education, they were heartily welcomed in Sunday schools. School sponsors actively sought opportunities to teach slaves and free blacks alike. Even in Southern states like South Carolina, Tennessee, and Missouri, Sunday classes served slaves as often as owners allowed. In northern cities like Philadelphia, Utica, and New York, from a quarter to two thirds of the adults who enrolled in Sunday schools around 1820 were black. Contemporary observers commented on the "intenseness of application" demonstrated by many of the black students given this chance to master words and the Word. And after the Civil War, the surge of black adults into Sunday schooling was massive.

From its launch, the Sunday-school movement was entwined with other charitable efforts to help the indigent. Many of the organizers, teachers, and donors were also active in groups like the Society for the Relief of Poor Women and Children, the Bowery Village Benevolent Society, Philadelphia Society for the Promotion of Public Economy, and similar groups that served

the poor. Teachers often handed out clothing, food, and other necessaries as part of their classes.

Precisely what kind of influence on the next generation did the reformers aim to have? A card that the Benton Street Mission Sunday School in St. Louis gave to parents is a typical document. Under the heading "What Our Sunday School Does" the aims of the school are summarized this way:

It trains children in the practice of benevolence, love, obedience to parents, truthfulness, kindness to one another, and purity of language. It seeks to lead them to love Jesus, and to walk in the path of wisdom.

One "path of wisdom" that nearly all Sunday schools taught to even their poorest children was the importance of being generous. Most schools collected small sums during the year to give to people in trouble and need. Eastern students might buy books for their counterparts in the less prosperous Midwest. Frontier students might give pennies to medical missionaries in India. A class would often adopt a single

In the first half of the nineteenth century, only about 50 percent of American children were given formal schooling. Many youngsters worked all day —like these Delaware newsgirls. Volunteer schools set up on the day of rest, Sunday, changed the lives of these children.

Sunday schools particularly sought out children and adults who lacked opportunities for learning. Free blacks and slaves were enrolled with enthusiasm, in great numbers.

cause or beneficiary and support it with steady little donations over a period of time. In addition to whatever practical help those funds provided, the practice established charitable human ties, and got the next generation of Americans used to the idea that everyone can, and should, offer assistance to others.

America's Sunday schools were surprisingly successful at avoiding religious battles, sectional rifts, or other jealousies that could have blocked their spread. Concerted effort was made to keep the Christian content of instructional materials broad enough to include all denominations. Sunday schools provided basic Bible teaching to all types of Protestants, Catholic families, and even people who did not believe in Christ. Records show that many schools were a mix of Methodists, Baptists, Presbyterians, Catholics, Episcopalians, Congregationalists, and others.

This charitable campaign's focus on the least, the lost, and the left-behind took an ambitious step forward in 1830, when delegates of the American Sunday School Union voted enthusiastically to push schools out across our nation's frontier. The annual meeting passed a Mississippi Valley Resolution pledging to organize, supply, and man Sunday schools "in every destitute place" across 1.3 million square miles of our Midwestern prairie. An outpouring of $60,000 in donations and a surge of volunteer teachers followed almost immediately. Three years later a similar pledge was made to spread schools across the South.

Those frontier Sunday schools became seminal institutions. For some settlers, the lessons were the only time they gathered with their scattered neighbors. Many families learned for the first time to write letters that connected them to friends and families back East. The seeds of Sunday schools sprouted into churches, common schools, and eventually villages. And a reservoir of basic literacy, shared religious knowledge, and Christian morality was created among the Americans manning the crude and sometimes cruel edges of our nascent civilization.

Thanks to energetic organizing, steady contributions, and vast expenditures of time by volunteer teachers, Sunday-school growth was meteoric. When the American Sunday School Union was founded in 1824 as a coordinating body, it attracted 723 local schools as members. Hundreds more schools belonged to some other local or regional group, or were unaffiliated. Just eight years later, the ASSU represented 8,268 schools. And by the time of the Civil War there were more than 60,000 schools.

Folding in the middle class

As their popularity boomed, Sunday-school classes expanded to include not only poor children but also most middle-class children. With common schools improving, Sunday schools began to move beyond basic reading instruction and focus on guiding their charges in how to live ethically, via Bible lessons and intensive mentoring from teachers. In most communities the two kinds of educational institutions were very aware of what the other was doing, and cooperated in ways that allowed each to be better and more specialized. Most families believed that children needed both kinds of training. Of children on the rolls of New York public schools in 1827, for instance, more than 60 percent also attended Sunday school.

It wasn't just parents who wanted Sunday schools to offer moral guidance. Many American leaders warned that the only way our experiment in popular government would succeed was if everyday people were educated and virtuous. In our urban slums and raw frontiers there were many individuals in serious need of elevation.

Most of the successful businessmen who funded the Sunday-school movement had risen from poverty by developing

Sunday-school organizers made "astonishing" progress in enrolling Native Americans, remote farm families, illiterate adults, and other underserved populations. Here is a Sunday-school class of Comanches at the Post Oak Mission in Oklahoma.

53

These "breaker boys," who worked in Pennsylvania mines separating coal from slate, were exactly the kind of children Sunday-school organizers targeted. "He will be a saint or a devil, and which of the two it may be for you to say."

wholesome disciplines. They knew what was needed by our strugglers, and how it could best be gotten. "We miss the heart of the problem if we neglect personal character and neighborhood righteousness," wrote one group of movement leaders.

A good glimpse into the mind and motivations of the American evangelical reformers who drove our Sunday-school crusade can be had from reading a sermon entitled "Our Sunday Schools and Our Country" that was delivered before a gathering of school managers in 1860, in New Haven, Connecticut. The name of the speaker has been lost to history, but he well encapsulated the purposes behind the work that thousands of volunteers put into this effort. He starts by invoking a society

distinguished not for its dazzling conquest, nor for the luxuries of princely wealth…but for that unity, liberty, and stability which are the fruits of a government that rests upon the intelligence and godliness of the people as its sure foundation…. How is this wisdom and this knowledge to be secured?

Not surely by legislative action, since no nation, however politically gifted, can enact themselves wise....

When you look upon a company of little ones… pause for a moment, and ask…. Who is that bright-eyed boy, in tattered dress, whom no kind friend has yet clothed?… He will be a *saint* or a *devil*, and which of the two, it may be for you to say. Somebody must take him by the hand and love him, and teach him to love, before hate gets the mastery of his heart….

But these children are to be something more than good citizens or bad citizens…. Immortality is the prerogative of the humblest of them…. They are to dwell with the lost, or to be "kings and priests to God."… How shall we fully meet the responsibility of such a relation, and faithfully do the duties belonging to it? The chief instrumentality for accomplishing all this is the Sunday school…. where mind, heart, and habit of life are all to be the subjects of the teacher's patient and devout labors.

The middle-class philanthropists behind the Sunday-school movement put emphasis on both individual integrity and social goodness, on personal success and on community harmony. They believed good moral instruction was the key to both. But they knew that in a country like America, the root of collective virtue would always be individual morality—the honesty, industry, and decency of each of society's members. So, as one historian notes, "by 1820 the Sunday school had joined the prayer meeting, the mission chapel, and the urban missionary as a tool for combating urban problems," with parallel efforts taking place across the wild prairies and forests of our frontier.

In European societies, religion was sometimes used as a tool to housebreak and control the poorer classes. And rulers everywhere are tempted to wield politics for that same purpose. The philanthropic reformers behind America's Sunday schools eschewed both of those approaches.

"Having rejected politics as a means to control the

The Brandywine Manufacturers' Sunday School was set up and operated by a combination of businessowners and laborers. It served thousands of children of all backgrounds, over a period of decades, out of this building.

Many poor children picked up more of their literacy, and their moral compass, at Sunday school than they did in our uneven, inadequate, and often nonexistent public schools.

Thousands of talented young volunteer Sunday-school teachers were the Teach For America cadre of their day. They not only provided literacy instruction and Bible training but also intensive mentoring that changed many children's lives (and deepened the convictions and talents of the volunteers).

lives of others, the men of the American Sunday School Union pursued a more elusive goal: Influence," writes historian Anne Boylan. "The Sunday school, while coercing no one, held up standards of conduct to which members could voluntarily submit…. It offered individuals a source of guidance and direction in a highly mobile society."

Americans, noted Sunday-school organizers, do not defer to "betters." If the schools were going to succeed, they could not be structured as places where middle-class and wealthy sponsors train poor children in obedience. They had to be places that enriched participants and were self-evidently desirable. So successful middle-class families put money and energy into providing this moral instruction for the young; and they also put in their own children.

From early on, business leaders, professionals, and prominent preachers like Lyman Beecher enrolled their offspring in the Sunday schools that also served poor and unchurched families. In 1817, the duPont family and other factory and mill owners in their region set up a Brandywine Manufacturers' Sunday School

that sat the children of workers and local farmers right next to the youngsters of company managers and bosses. DuPont's daughters volunteered in classrooms every week as teachers. Even the school trustees were a mix of manual workers and superintendents from the mills. Similar mixings of social classes could be seen in Sunday schools operating in New England, Pennsylvania, upstate New York, and elsewhere.

In this way, Sunday schooling became a mass phenomenon. By 1920 there were 200,000 Sunday schools in the country. Tens of millions of young and old Americans received instruction every year.

Harnessing the power of committed teachers
The Sunday-school movement's most potent asset was its cadre of volunteer teachers. Most were enthusiastic young adults just a decade or so older than their students. Think of them as the talented Teach For America instructors of their era.

It was determined from the beginning that teachers should strive to be mentors and role models, not just instructors. Toward this end, classes were kept at intimate sizes—about ten pupils per leader. And it was standard procedure for teachers to visit students in their homes and build "strong reciprocal affections" that often led to long-term associations. In addition to their class time, teachers went on excursions with students, visited them when they were sick, and took an interest in their lives. Lots of correspondence survives to document the respect and friendship and behavior-modeling that often developed between teachers and charges. Thanks to these personal bonds, when the storms of adolescence raged it was generally true that "the last cord snapped will be the Sunday-school teacher's influence."

Here again we come across that gentle word "influence." The warm relations between teacher and child that bolstered the character-shaping power of the Sunday school were different from the dynamic that existed in most public schools. For one thing, Sunday schools prohibited corporal punishment. In an era when there was lots of whipping and caning and rodding in common schools, the organizers of Sunday schools insisted that "kindness alone"

should discipline the children, that "persuasion forms the only weapon of the teacher."

Obviously this wasn't easy. Teachers sometimes faced rather feral children whom they had to reprimand for lying, cruelty, swearing, and other behaviors that needed to change. Yet their success levels were surprisingly high. There are many community testimonials like the report from New Jersey attesting that "no sooner were schools commenced in destitute places than a change was visible in the morals of the children and the inhabitants of the neighborhood."

A final way that some Sunday-school pupils emulated their admired mentors was by joining them in the teaching corps. This was sufficiently common to create a self-fueling mechanism for the schools. The most important element that made them work—their volunteer leaders—replenished itself.

"Throughout most of the nineteenth century, Sunday schools were the only American institutions for children that relied entirely on volunteer labor for their maintenance and perpetuation," notes Boylan. The very first Sunday schools set up

The only way our experiment in popular government would succeed, many American leaders warned, was if everyday people were educated and virtuous.

The Chautauqua gatherings, a direct outgrowth of the Sunday-schooling movement, became a powerful influence on America—building our tradition of constant self-improvement and lifelong learning.

By 1920 there were 200,000 Sunday schools, and tens of millions of young and old Americans received instruction every year.

by philanthropists in the 1790s actually employed paid teachers, with less impressive results. But amidst thousands of personal religious conversions during the Second Great Awakening, waves of volunteer teachers emerged. Starting around 1810 they poured themselves into the schools, creating one of the most impressive successes of voluntarism in American history.

Teachers believed this was important mission work. And many were also attracted for personal reasons. One of the secret powers of the Sunday-school movement was that at the same time it lifted and formed its students, it also gratified teachers and fed their souls.

"The lives of Sunday-school teachers, as pictured in diaries and memoirs, reveal the significance they attached to teaching," writes Boylan. These young adults, most newly born again in their faith, found that this work helped cement their Christianity identity, and meshed well with their youthful search for meaning.

There were also lots of opportunities for Sunday-school teachers to get together for social interaction and fun—picnics, boatrides, singing, etc.—and for the exchanges of information

and mutual reinforcement that build esprit de corps. Scads of magazines and advice books were published specifically for Sunday-school teachers. These not only spread effective techniques and encouragement, but built solidarity across boundaries of denomination, region, and so forth that could have slowed this work if not overcome.

Most of these young leaders were very serious about mastering their craft. In order to "preserve their own self-respect and the respect of their pupils," urged one participant, Sunday-school teachers should strive to equal or exceed the effectiveness of professional teachers working in the common schools, "not only in breadth of mind but in capacity to instruct." There were publications that taught teachers Greek and Hebrew so they could be more effective Bible interpreters. The latest assessments of effective classroom technique were shared across the teaching corps. Teachers gathered in regular prayer meetings and reinforced each other. In the second half of the 1800s a whole network of "teachers' institutes" grew up across the country, to train Sabbath teachers in the best techniques and information.

Princeton professor Archibald Alexander observed that lots of young Sunday-school teachers were "actually becoming accurate Bible theologians." Major New York philanthropist John Pintard observed to a correspondent that his stepgrandson, who had taken up teaching, was "deriving more Bible information" from his Sunday-school volunteering "than left to himself he would probably have acquired all his life." Many instructors commented on how teaching had enriched their own understanding. "How often, while we have been endeavoring to instill into the children's minds a knowledge," wrote one Baltimore woman, "have our own hearts been made to burn within us."

Hitting human chords

One side effect of America's Sunday-school mobilization was the Chautauqua movement. Two Methodists—minister John Vincent and entrepreneur Lewis Miller—wanted to offer information, practical training, and inspiration to the men and women staffing Sunday schools. So they and other philanthropists created a kind of summer camp-meeting on the shore of lovely Chautauqua Lake in western

New York and invited young teachers from across the East and Midwest to come hear lectures, participate in book groups, sing hymns, study the history and geography of the Holy Land, and refresh themselves through dips in the lake, woodland walks, and friendly dinners with fellow teachers and Christians who were aiming to sharpen their minds and hone their teaching skills in exactly the same ways.

The original Chautauqua assemblies were so popular and so successful at disseminating knowledge and moral enthusiasm across the country that they were copied in hundreds of other places. The self-improving holiday became an American tradition, and "chautauqua" became a generic term in our language, defined as "a series of adult education courses and entertainments held outdoors in the summer for purposes of self-improvement." Americans' attraction to this kind of earnest instructional recreation and the whole concept of lifelong learning—which can be seen today in everything from TED talks to self-help guides to neighborhood book circles—was in many ways first crystallized in the Chautauqua gatherings.

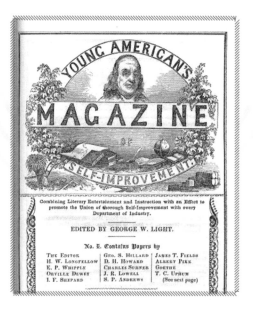

The Sunday-school movement created a boom in book and magazine publishing and library-making for children, including the first Christian-inflected juvenile fiction and music, created to make moral learning captivating.

Businessmen played a large role in organizing Sunday schooling, and this showed up in the movement's effective marketing—advertisements like this card that was handed out on the street, billboards, book giveaways, use of rooms near the target audience, and other details of savvy management.

Sunday schooling also became a force in publishing. Not only study plans and Bible lessons but also popular magazines, children's stories, novels, and morality tales that were avidly absorbed by millions of adolescents and young adults flew off the presses, with support from philanthropists. A whole culture of reading grew out of Sunday schooling, and historians report that this was a prime factor in making American laborers the most literate in the world.

As early as 1829, the American Sunday School Union (which was just one of many publishers that competed to supply classrooms) reported it had issued more than 5 million copies of various publications over the previous five years. This required printing 100,000 pages every day. A genre of Christian fiction for children was created and distributed through Sunday schools, at a time when fiction was dismissed by many Americans as useless or even harmful. Movement leaders

were wise enough to understand that stories that pull children to the printed word both train their brains and open opportunities to inform appetites and values. Sunday-school fiction was crafted to make reading fun, even addictive, while transmitting wholesome ideas.

All of this output not only required the movement's leaders to master new technology for mass communication, but also to marshal new forms of creativity. Stables of freelance writers had to be built up to fill the magazines, write the study guides, and craft the new Christian fiction. Ministers and professional teachers were often recruited as writers. Certain authors became prolific, sometimes presiding over workshops of acolytes who churned out works.

Teachers often gave away books and periodicals as prizes. Sunday schools also built up remarkable lending libraries. By 1832, there were about 4,000 Sunday schools with libraries that children could borrow from, and the average collection contained around 100 books. Libraries became even commoner, and larger, as the years passed, and these helped prepare many children for life in a nation where reading was becoming essential to success. The Sunday-school reading material also transmitted a whole complex of Protestant virtues, personal disciplines, and moral perspectives that equipped poor children to move quickly into America's burgeoning middle class.

Sunday-school philanthropists harnessed the power of new forms of popular culture in other areas as well. In 1810, there were few songs created specifically for children and teenagers, and none but a handful that had any educational or moral content. Movement leaders went to work to change that, insisting that there "is no reason the devil should have all the popular tunes."

Sunday schools gave out sheet music, books, magazines, and printed pictures to students as rewards. They sponsored picnics and field trips. They distributed food and clothing to threadbare students. Free classes in sewing and other practical skills were offered. Employment agencies were created at some urban Sunday schools to connect families to work. It's no surprise Sunday school became a highlight of many childhoods.

A charity run by businessmen
Much of this savvy marketing stemmed from the fact that

businessmen were the main organizers and funders of the Sunday-school movement. The largest umbrella organization, the American Sunday School Union, has been referred to as "a society run by merchants." Commercial skill was apparent in many of the organizational methods that helped make the movement successful.

While they firmly believed that "Christian character, earnestness, and love for souls" were the essential bedrock of successful Sunday schooling, the businessmen who led the effort recognized "the necessity for practical efficiency" if they were going to have a chance of transforming the nation. So they were not shy about advertising Sunday-school publications on the flyleaves of popular new books and children's magazines. They put together special five-dollar and ten-dollar Sunday School Libraries that could be ordered as a kit. They printed flyers to market Sunday schools and distributed them in streetcars.

"At a time when the United States had few national institutions, virtually no national communications network (except the U.S. mail, which these men molded to their needs), and no national corporations, the

The American enthusiasm for self-improvement and lifelong learning—which can be seen today in everything from TED talks to self-help guides to neighborhood book circles— was first crystallized by the Sunday-school movement.

Arthur Tappan and other donors paid for a massive effort to establish Sunday schools all across isolated and lonely spots of America's frontier West, where the philanthropists felt the need was greatest and the payoff to the nation highest. Here are rural Minnesota Sunday schoolers dressed in their best.

management of the American Sunday School Union established the framework for what was, in effect, a national evangelical corporation," summarizes Boylan.

Who were these leaders? The first wave included prominent philanthropists like Benjamin Rush and Theodore Gallaudet. A little later, important roles were played by war-horse donors of the Second Great Awakening like Gerrit Smith and Arthur Tappan (who provided the seed money for the Mississippi Valley campaign).

The men who really ramped things up, though, were evangelical Christian entrepreneurs who had left small towns and farms to participate in America's commercial boom during the 1800s. They were eager that other poor citizens should have a chance to rise as they did. And they worried that the moral behaviors necessary for personal and national success were not consistently taught to the young.

Alexander Henry ran a thriving import business, and became the first president of the American Sunday School Union. John Brown was a financier who founded Brown Brothers investment bank and gave devoted volunteer service and a lifetime of donations to Sunday schools, then left $10,000 to the cause when he died. There were china merchants, flour millers, manufacturers, and shoemakers among the movement's leadership.

Most funders were also volunteer leaders who gave the effort its strategy and techniques, and many were involved at a grassroots level in their own community schools. John Wanamaker, the genius retailer famous for his honesty and his pioneering deployment of advertising, personally set up a collection of Sunday schools in poor neighborhoods of Philadelphia. Francis Scott Key, the lawyer who penned our national anthem, was a serious Christian who taught Bible classes for years, then helped guide the American Sunday School Union. The Brandywine Manufacturers' Sunday School that was staffed and funded partly by the duPont family taught an average of 200 students for decades.

Rooting the Protestant ethic in American breasts

The giant push made by these philanthropists to teach Americans to read and instruct them in the Christian faith and the habits of self-mastery was a smash success—for pupils, teachers, neighbors, and the nation. Sunday schools became both community fixtures and creators of American identity. "On the frontier, mission schools brought the familiar rituals and symbols of Protestant life to newly settled areas," explains Boylan. "Urban mission schools delivered important social services to pupils and their families through employment agencies, free classes, and winter relief."

"The Sunday school was not just for children," she continues. "It served, as one missionary noted, as a 'central point where all in the neighborhood meet to teach or be taught.'" And "most churches of the West of recent formation have grown out of Sunday schools previously existing," commented one 1859 observer.

Sunday schools also birthed or fueled other social innovations. The YMCA movement, for instance, and the Christian Commission that was active during the Civil War were each created and manned by many of the same volunteers and donors powering Sunday schools. Both of those organizations were important in helping young people, especially new urbanites, adapt to drastic changes in American life without losing their moral compasses. And many of the businessmen and clerks who became the main constituents of the YMCA movement were in turn encouraged to teach at Sunday schools as part of their service to community.

The Benton Street Mission in St. Louis, the Railroad Mission in Chicago, Dwight Moody's school, the North End Mission in Boston, Bethany Mission in Philadelphia—these all grew out of Sunday schooling, and became full-service neighborhood charities providing everything from cheap restaurants to shelter for reformed prostitutes. "On frontiers both rural and urban, the school became the advance guard for the introduction of other 'civilizing' institutions, especially the church and the common school," concludes Boylan, "but also the central values of Protestant culture, including self-discipline, benevolence, orderliness, and self-improvement. Seen in the broad context of cultural extension, the schools' educational importance can hardly be overstated." ⬆

As "agencies of cultural transmission," Sunday schools—run by devoted young role models, and organized and funded by volunteer businessmen—were enormously influential in cementing virtues like self-discipline, benevolence, and self-improvement.

— A CASE STUDY —

Changing Society through Civil Action

Abolition

There have been principled objections to slavery for as long as there has been slavery—which is to say, from the first days of human history. But hatred of enslavement didn't become a mass conviction until Christian philanthropists in Britain and America got deeply involved in popular campaigns to expose slavery as an ugly, immoral, and sinful activity, utterly incompatible with life in a free land. This was demanding and dangerous work that required guile, endurance, commitment, courage, managerial genius, and money. The movement got all of these things from leaders like Arthur and Lewis Tappan.

Fired by their deep evangelical Christian convictions, the Tappan brothers were leading providers of strategy and funding to the cause of abolishing slavery. (They also powered many other important social reforms. For some biography on the men, see the last third of the case study on the Second Great Awakening.) Arthur was the lead funder and visionary, and Lewis the vital organizer, behind creation of the American Anti-Slavery Society. Starting from nothing in 1833, the AASS quickly became the largest and most effective culture-change organization in American history.

Leaders of the charity brilliantly orchestrated massive shifts in public sentiment.

Organizing culture change

Culture change is not for cowards, and abolitionists were bullied from the moment they first stuck their heads up.

As part of their broader effort to refine Americans through worship, education, discussion, and service, Arthur and Lewis Tappan had in 1832 leased a tatterdemalion old theater in lower Manhattan and converted it into a church. The building "squatted in the midst of the slums" next to Five Points, a neighborhood notorious for its gangs and grog shops. During recent years the theater had been home to a circus, and with his sharp nose for drama and public interest, Lewis noted that "the *sensation* produced by converting the place with slight alterations into a church will be very great, and curiousity will be excited."

The Tappans placed their Chatham Street Chapel at the disposal of Charles Grandison Finney—a powerful public speaker, former lawyer, and Presbyterian minister who had recently led a series of phenomenally large and passionate religious revivals across upstate New York and other parts of the country, bringing the boiler of the Second Great Awakening to its peak steam. In addition to the large services attracted by Finney, the chapel was made available to other groups of black and white worshipers, as a venue for religious music concerts, and as a public lecture and meeting location for various charitable associations the Tappans supported, including the first national convention of the U.S. Sunday-school movement (see companion case study) and many abolitionist gatherings.

Large-scale organizing of anti-slavery societies began, as things often do in America, at the state level. The New York Anti-Slavery Society was created at a meeting the Tappan brothers arranged at Chatham Street Chapel on October 2, 1833. And before the charity was two hours old, a riot broke out.

The new society was having a respectably dull democratic birth—written constitution adopted, officers elected (Arthur Tappan was chosen as president)—when a mob tried to snatch up the baby and bash its brains out. When they heard that an anti-slavery association was being organized in the city,

a group of opponents posted handbills and gathered a crowd for a counter-meeting. Whipped into a frenzy by speechifiers, the assemblage turned to angry protest. They streamed out of Tammany Hall, where they had convened, and surged a few blocks to the Chatham Street Chapel, where they broke up that inaugural meeting of New York City anti-slavers. At least one drunken rioter pursued Arthur and Lewis Tappan into the darkness with a lantern and dagger, but allies hustled the reformers away.

The brothers were not cowed. Arthur funded a new abolitionist newspaper called the *Emancipator*. He provided grants to set up anti-slavery societies in other states. He and Lewis were sparkplugs behind the convening of the first national convention of abolitionists. At that gathering, in Philadelphia, a Declaration of Sentiments was approved, and the American Anti-Slavery Society was launched to coordinate civil actions aimed at ending human bondage on our shores.

Philanthropists across the country started to publicize simple moral arguments against enforced servitude:

This painting depicts slaves waiting to be sold. The fact that slavery broke up families was one of the arguments used to turn hatred of enslavement into a mass conviction.

American philanthropists engineered a range of popular campaigns that exposed slavery as an ugly, immoral, and sinful activity, utterly incompatible with life in a free land. This was demanding and dangerous work.

CHATHAM THEATRE.

The Tappan brothers acquired an old circus theater and turned it into an evangelical church where people of all races and persuasions were gathered to worship, and to fight for social reforms like temperance, Sunday schooling, and the abolition of slavery. It became a flash point for violent opponents.

- No one, they insisted, has the right to buy and sell other human beings.
- It is wrong for slaveowners to be able to severely punish and even kill a slave without trial.
- Parents should never have their children taken away from them and sold.

- Husbands and wives should be legally married and protected from involuntary separation.
- The pattern of planters making concubines of slaves is sinful and abusive.
- Laws prohibiting education of the enslaved must be repealed.

- It's immoral that slaves should be blocked from practicing organized faith.

A great crusade had begun.

Violence against freedom

As prominent merchants, famous backers of benevolent groups, and now chief donors and organizers of slavery-fighting charities, the Tappan brothers had a high profile in New York City. Vicious rumors were spread about their aims and practices, and those of their philanthropic allies. It was claimed that Arthur Tappan had divorced his wife and taken up with a black woman. It was said that abolitionists wanted to dissolve the Union, that they sought "racial mongrelization," that they were going to violate the Constitution.

On a hot July 4, seven months after the founding of the American Anti-Slavery Society, Lewis Tappan opened the Chatham Street Chapel to a racially mixed congregation for a special worship service. Tappan himself gave a "forcible and impressive" presentation of abolitionist principles. Then white and black choirs began to sing a new anti-slavery hymn written for the occasion by John Greenleaf Whittier. But slavery apologists had infiltrated the balcony, and now they rained down prayer books and hymnals from above. Stomping, hissing, and fighting, they drove the worshipers away.

The pro-slavery press celebrated the action, and published more calumny about what the Anti-Slavery Society and its backers were up to. A few days later, bullies were back at the chapel, throwing benches, trashing the premises, and beating bystanders. They traveled a short distance across lower Manhattan to Lewis Tappan's home at 40 Rose Street and yelled for him to come out, before finally dispersing.

The next evening, a mob of several thousand people gathered on the streets and began to maraud. The violence was observed and even orchestrated by some leading citizens. A well-dressed man on a horse led the crowd back to Tappan's house on Rose Street. Lewis was warned that trouble was on the way and he and his family fled. The rabble broke down his front door, smashed windows, and entered and vandalized the home. They dragged all of the family's personal possessions—clothing, pictures, furniture, personal papers, and so forth—into the street and set them on fire. Arthur observed the destruction of his brother's domicile from the nearby shadows.

Some observers suggest the house was saved from even more complete destruction by a spasm of rectitude among the rabble. It seems a portrait of George Washington was one of the items torn from the family walls and handed out to the street. Someone observed that it was an image of the father of our country and shrieked, "for God's sake, don't burn Washington." The cry rippled through the ranks of the brawlers: "For God's sake, don't burn Washington!," and there was a lull in the violence. A later writer recorded that "in an instant, the spirit of disorder was laid, and the portrait handed carefully from man to man, til, at length, the populace carried it to a neighboring house for safety," attended by an honor guard of rioters. About then, a group of watchmen and firefighters arrived, and the mob was driven off.

But the next day they were out again, smashing black and white abolitionist churches, beating blacks on the street, and threatening to destroy Chatham Street Chapel, offices of abolitionist publications, and homes of other white donors and leaders. They roared up to the three-story warehouse and store run by the Tappan brothers at 122 Pearl Street, on Hanover Square, where they beat police trying to guard the premises, pummeled the building with rocks, and attempted to batter in the front door with a street pole. But it was a heavy granite building, and Arthur Tappan had holed up inside with some clerks and friends—to whom he handed out 36 muskets, with orders to shoot low and disable anyone entering. When a watchman told the attackers as he was being stabbed and beaten that the building was full of armed men, the invasion halted.

Other rioters sought out Arthur Tappan at his lodgings, but found the premises guarded by soldiers. By now the Tammany Democrats who had helped foment the anti-abolitionist uproar were concerned that the violence was out of control and could threaten prosperous allies, so they belatedly called in cavalry troops and infantry, and placed the city under martial law. Police and soldiers flooded Manhattan. They were told to deal leniently with the ruffians, though, and most of the 150 leaders of the multiday violence who were arrested got quickly released by political authorities.

In the anti-abolition riots that swept New York City in 1834, thousands of ruffians, egged on by slavery apologists in city government, the media, and commercial classes, attacked a range of targets: philanthropists, their homes, and their places of business; black residents; and churches, including the Chatham Street Chapel.

Within months of the founding of the American Anti-Slavery Society, rioters were attacking the homes and businesses of its charitable backers.

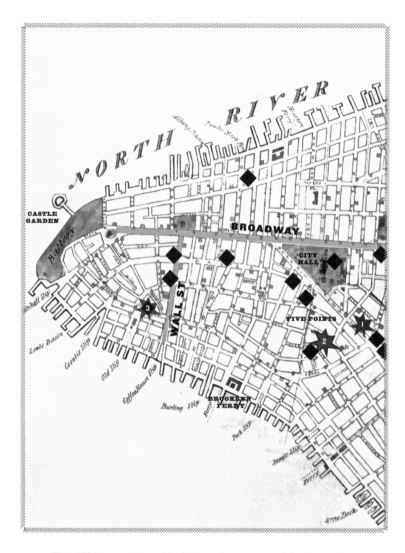

This 1834 map of lower Manhattan shows some of the sites where marauding gangs attacked abolitionists and their religious, commercial, and charitable institutions. The star labeled 1 is the Chatham Street Chapel, where some of the earliest attacks began. The star labeled 2 is Lewis Tappan's house, which was demolished by the mob, including almost all of his family's personal possessions. The star labeled 3 is the Tappan brothers' silk business, where Arthur saved the building from destruction by holing up inside with 36 friends armed with muskets. Other sites are churches or homes that were assaulted.

The great mailing campaign

New York's political establishment and pro-slavery elements of the press initially tried to airbrush this anti-abolitionist violence. The destruction of Lewis Tappan's home was described in the *Courier* and *Enquirer* newspapers as a peaceful demonstration by some gentlemen, in the course of which a window was broken. To put the lie to this false reporting Lewis announced he was going to leave the ruined shell of his house, strewn with his destroyed personal possessions and those of his wife and children, exactly as the attackers left things, to serve as a "silent anti-slavery preacher to the crowds who will flock to see it." With his vivid sense for public sentiment, he recognized that his personal misfortune provided an opportunity to advertise his cause, and the cruelty of those who opposed it. His wife, Susan, was similarly brave and stoic, joking with her husband as she viewed the wreckage that the events had pared away some furnishings he had never liked anyway.

The final accounting from the riot, though, was no joke. Seven churches and a dozen houses had been wrecked. Fires smoldered across southern Manhattan. Scores of private citizens had been beaten, and many police and members of the 27th Regiment of Infantry had been clubbed, stoned, or stabbed.

This became national news. Descriptions of how white and black advocates of ending slavery were being violently persecuted spread across the country. The same stories outlined the principles of the new national and state-level Anti-Slavery Societies, and precisely how their members hoped to change America.

Despite their narrow escapes, both of the Tappan brothers were undeterred. Arthur immediately put up the money to have 15,000 copies of a special installment of the *Emancipator* circulated. One ally observed that in the aftermath of the riots Arthur Tappan's "whole soul never seemed so enlisted." Lewis too was invigorated by the danger. His only defensive reaction was to start carrying a copy of the New Testament in his breast pocket. After one of the Manhattan pro-slavery newspapers suggested that local residents were ready "to give him a second lesson in public manners," he wrote that "the Lord, we trust, will overrule this 'madness of the people.'"

In the weeks after the 1834 riot, the two brothers and their abolitionist allies resolved to fight back. Except they would use words rather than battering rams and stones. They made a plan to flood the U.S. with anti-slavery mailings.

These philanthropists founded, expanded, and subsidized a host of weekly and monthly publications devoted to popularizing arguments against enslavement. These included high-circulation newspapers, a children's magazine (which Lewis Tappan headed up himself as it was being created), a more philosophical journal, and a heavily illustrated monthly. With extensive volunteer labor, these publications and others were churned out in volume on new steam-powered presses, and then staged at New York City post offices to be hurried across the country. The campaign was powered by $30,000 of personal donations pledged to the American Anti-Slavery Society.

The abolitionists called this their effort in "moral suasion." The National Postal Museum has described it as America's first-ever direct-mail campaign. It was certainly one of the most ambitious polemical blitzes ever conducted in our country. The main targets of the mailings were ministers, local legislators, businessmen, and judges living all across the country, including in the South. Barely one year after the 1834 riots, the American Anti-Slavery Society's publications committee, headed by Lewis Tappan, had the first batch of newspapers, magazines, journals, and pamphlets ready—175,000 separate items delivered to the main New York City post office in large piles. From then on, at least 25,000 copies of each publication rolled off the presses each week, and over the next ten months the society mailed out a total of more than a million pieces of anti-slavery literature.

Speaking and authoring

This mail blitz was just the most visible prong of the moral suasion campaign. At the same time, the American Anti-Slavery Society launched special efforts to woo ministers. Anti-slavery materials were printed up for use by the Sunday schools beginning to burgeon across the land. Among the hundreds of thousands of new Christian converts then being mobilized by Charles Finney and other revivalists, the society promoted the idea that slavery and complicity with slavery is a sin. Scores of church associations and denominational groups went on record with that position, and evangelical Christians began to shift *en masse* into the "immediate abolition" camp.

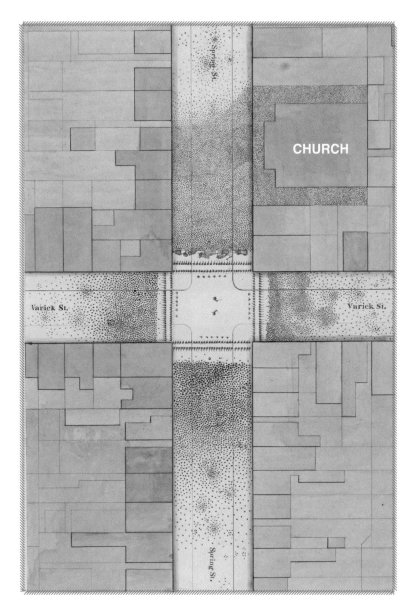

This historic drawing, from the archives of the Museum of the City of New York, depicts thousands of rioters (the tiny black dots) as they pillage an abolitionist church on Spring Street and other sites, despite efforts to secure the nearby street intersection made by 27th Regiment soldiers (who were belatedly called out by the mayor, and are depicted in double bayoneted lines).

THE
SLAVE'S FRIEND

VOL. II. No. XII.   WHOLE No. 24.

AN AFFECTING STORY.
[*From the Western Christian Advocate.*]

Jack is a Methodist local preacher. In one of his sermons he told this story. "When I was a lad there were no religious people near where I lived. But I had

The Slave's Friend was a magazine for children created by Lewis Tappan and other philanthropists after his house was demolished by slavery apologists. It was one part of a massive campaign to print and mail abolitionist arguments to families and opinion leaders all across the country.

Meantime, the Tappans and other leaders of the AASS created a program that hired gifted lecturers to go on public-speaking tours across the country presenting the case against slavery. To coordinate the effort they enlisted a brilliant young man named Theodore Weld, whom the Tappans had previously funded to establish schools in upstate New York and then Ohio for training the next generation of Christian reformers. Weld and three other men undertook so dense a schedule of public speeches that within two years he had damaged his voice for life.

When it became clear how effective the itinerant speakers were, Weld was charged with recruiting and training a full cadre of 70 lecturers and then sending them roving across the nation. He did his job well, and these 70 orators—described by Lyman Beecher as the "he-goat men… butting everything in the line of their march…made up of vinegar, aqua fortis, and oil of vitriol, with brimstone, saltpeter and charcoal to explode and scatter the corrosive matter"—soon became famous for helping bring this first bloom of abolitionism to a climax during 1836 and 1837.

As soon as he got his public speakers dispatched across small-town America, Theodore Weld jumped into another project funded by the American Anti-Slavery Society's donors. He methodically combed through thousands of installments of Southern newspapers, public speeches, and facts and figures to collect true accounts of the real-life treatment of slaves. How are they disciplined? What about if they become ill? What happens to their families when they are sold? Runaways get what sort of treatment?

Weld condensed his documentary snippets into a simple but repellently rich book entitled *American Slavery As It Is: Testimony of a Thousand Witnesses.* The volume made waves after it was published by the AASS in 1839 and distributed from the charitable society's headquarters on Nassau Street in New York. And it had an even more climactic effect when it became the major background source for the bestselling novel *Uncle Tom's Cabin.* The cultural power of that work by Harriet Beecher Stowe is captured in Lincoln's description of her, when they first met, as "the little woman who wrote the book that made this great war."

Opponents—and government—lash out

This moral-suasion campaign absolutely maddened apologists for slavery. In particular, the circulation of abolitionist arguments through the federal mail hit a nerve. Anti-slavery mailings began to be methodically pulled out of post offices and burned. Threats were floated against anyone who subscribed. The U.S. Postmaster General gave aid and comfort to local postmasters who abetted these acts of censorship and intimidation. Indeed, U.S. President Andrew Jackson actively encouraged postal authorities to suppress deliveries of all abolitionist documents, or at least look the other way while others did. In his 1835 message to Congress, Jackson called for a national censorship law that would shut down the charitable mailings of "incendiary" writings, and severely punish the men organizing them. Legislation was not passed, but the officially encouraged vigilante actions effectively halted the distribution of abolitionist arguments within the South.

Up to this point in American history, historians like Kathleen McCarthy note, defenders of slavery had "kept the leavening potential of civil society in check…watchfully curbing any trend which might contribute to the development of alternative, independent power bases." But now they were faced with a savvy and well-funded mass charitable campaign that educated people and mobilized volunteers in opposition to their interests.

So when this flood of exhortation in favor of freedom crested across the country, the enemies of abolition lashed out. Arthur Tappan was hung in effigy in town squares, as torches were put to piles of newspapers and magazines. Lewis was mailed a slave's ear, a hangman's rope, and many written threats. A Virginia grand jury indicted him and other members of the American Anti-Slavery Society. Offers of $30,000 and $50,000 were made for delivery of Arthur's or Lewis's head to Louisiana. A South Carolinian raised the bid to $100,000 for Arthur. After hearing of these prizes, Arthur was reported to have said in an uncommon moment of humor that "if that sum is placed in a New York bank, I may possibly think of giving myself up." The mayor of Brooklyn stationed police patrols in front of Arthur's house to deter

Harriet Beecher Stowe's bestselling novel *Uncle Tom's Cabin* had a powerful effect on U.S. public opinion, leading President Lincoln to describe her as "the little woman who wrote the book that made this great war." She drew most of her background material from the non-fiction exposé *American Slavery As It Is*, created and published by the American Anti-Slavery Society with charitable donations.

The massive "moral suasion" effort that philanthropists funded to blizzard abolitionist literature across the country is described by the National Postal Museum as America's first-ever direct-mail campaign.

It unhinged defenders of slavery, whose backlash led to invasions of the mail (above), rewards for killing Arthur Tappan, and attempts at censorship by members of government extending all the way up to President Andrew Jackson. These brutal reactions turned many Americans permanently against slavery.

assassins, and a military force was organized at the Brooklyn Navy Yard to prevent kidnappers from carrying him away in a pilot boat headed for the South, as had been rumored.

"Frequently in times of crisis, hatreds focus upon a single individual who comes to symbolize all that is thought evil," comments Wyatt-Brown. For a period, the arch nemesis of slavery's defenders was philanthropist Arthur Tappan. Many establishment figures without a strong position on slavery also put pressure on the Tappan brothers to stand down for expedient reasons. At one point a delegation of city dignitaries and leaders of the New York Chamber of Commerce trooped into the Tappan store to complain to the brothers that

their organizing was damaging the business of merchants who depended on southern trade. "You demand that I shall cease my anti-slavery labors?" spluttered Arthur. "*I will be hung first!*"

The Tappans weren't hung, but they did become financial martyrs to their cause. Starting in Charleston, dry-goods dealers organized a boycott of the Tappan wholesaling operation. This was one of the first organized attempts to damage a national business because of the moral and political convictions of its proprietors. It would not be the last. A "vigilance committee" in Nashville and newspapers in Virginia urged local businessmen and citizens to punish the Tappan's firm in every way possible. Southern buyers walked away from their debts to Arthur Tappan and Company, and Southern lawyers refused to pursue the delinquents in court.

Victims, and victors

There were many other serious victims. A seminary student named Amos Dresser was publicly whipped in Nashville when he was discovered to be carrying a copy of the *Emancipator* in his luggage. For "circulating Tappan papers," Dr. Reuben Crandall was thrown in jail in Georgetown, then a separate city in the District of Columbia. Blacks in many places were attacked without provocation. Elizur Wright, who edited several of the publications mailed by the AASS, was besieged in his house by a mob that aimed to kidnap him and whisk him off to North Carolina. Publisher William Lloyd Garrison had to be locked by the mayor inside the Boston jailhouse to save him from violence at the hands of a raging pack. Abolitionist donors Gerrit Smith and Lewis Tappan were harassed while in Utica.

For publishing the anti-slavery *Philanthropist* in Cincinnati, printer James Birney had his press thrown into the Ohio River. When a mob in Philadelphia discovered abolitionist materials on a wharf awaiting shipment, they dumped them into the Delaware River. In Alton, Illinois, a local printer of abolitionist literature named Elijah Lovejoy was shot and killed while defending his press. At one of the large churches he had established in New York City, Lewis Tappan organized a memorial service for Lovejoy, and a special 40,000-copy edition of *Human Rights,* an AASS periodical, was published to catalogue the crime.

Theodore Weld thundered against the censure and lynchings and intimidation. "The empty name of freedom is everywhere—free government, free men, free people, free schools, and free churches. Hollow counterfeits all!…Rome's loudest shout for liberty was when she murdered it…. Free! The word and sound are omnipresent masks, and mockers! An impious lie!"

William Jay, son of founding father and first U.S. Supreme Court chief justice John Jay, commented on how dramatically the abolition struggle had been transformed by the Southern backlash against the Tappans' mailing campaign.

> We commenced the present struggle to obtain the freedom of the slave; we are compelled to continue it to preserve our own. We are now contending, not so much with the slaveholders of the South about human rights, as with the political and commercial aristocracy of the North for the liberty of speech, of the press, and of conscience.

Though elites remained skittish, the hearts and minds of many middle-class Northerners were won by the anti-slavery forces amidst this struggle. The attacks on the New York City homes and churches, the violation of the mail, the suppression of speech in American precincts, the attempts to have the Tappans and other advocates extradited to the South, the many acts of thuggish violence by slavery apologists— these actions turned large chunks of public opinion, especially among Northern churchgoers, firmly against slavery. The South's refusal to even tolerate discussion on slavery was exposed for the first time, along with the ugly behavior of slavery apologists. The pro-slavery response to the great mailing campaign, wrote Elizur Wright, "has done more than could have been by the arguments of a thousand agents to convince the sober and disinterested" of slavery's vicious effects on all who traffic in it.

The rioters and mail burners who were hoping to suppress the American Anti-Slavery Society and intimidate its charitable backers had exactly the opposite effect. In

William Jay, son of Founding Father John Jay and himself a prominent jurist and philanthropist, noted that the violent rebuffs of slavers to charitable attempts at persuasion pushed defenders of "liberty of speech, of the press, and of conscience" into sympathy with the abolitionist cause.

DECLARATION OF THE ANTI-SLAVERY CONVENTION.

Philanthropists created a host of new advocacy techniques— steam printing, lecture tours, cultivation of pastors, fundraising craft shows, monthly concerts, and so forth—to move public opinion.

the year after Lewis Tappan's home was invaded, 15,000 Americans bought new subscriptions to AASS publications. Anti-slavery societies began to spread like wildfire all across the country. There were 200 chapters in 1835, then 527 a year later, and 1,400 just two years further on. In an era of difficult communications, the American Anti-Slavery Society had by then enrolled 250,000 paying members—a full 2 percent of our national population. In comparative terms, that made the AASS bigger than today's Boy Scouts, or National Rifle Association, or Chamber of Commerce. For the first time, philanthropists had turned abolition into a major popular crusade, and slavery was now a subject no American could ignore.

The techniques of abolition advocacy

Lewis Tappan received a letter from his brother Benjamin, whose politics and faith were quite different, complaining about a billboard-style campaign against problem drinking that Lewis and other evangelicals had sponsored. Lewis replied with good-humored vigor that "you infidels should keep up with the age. This is a century of inventions."

The techniques of advocacy that Lewis and his allies pioneered and then employed to great effect changed the country in many ways in the three decades prior to the Civil War. Creating associations, sponsoring petitions, distributing handbills, holding conventions, circulating ideas for sermons, organizing nationwide speaking tours, creating Sunday schools and their curricula, publishing periodicals and pamphlets in large numbers and then distributing them by a combination of subscription and free mailing to culture-influencers—these and other techniques fueled by a mix of devoted volunteer time and steady private donations had deep effects on both grassroots and establishment opinion.

Before he shifted his patriotic energies (in concert with many other evangelical businessmen of his time) from often-frustrating political action to the more entrepreneurial work of culture change, Lewis had been involved as a young man in Federalist politics. He learned during that foray to avoid negativity, snobbery, and obstructionism. Such techniques, he found, annoyed and felt unpatriotic to many average Americans.

So instead, inspiring monthly concerts and prayer meetings for the enslaved were organized in parlors and churches all across the country on the first Monday. Very popular fundraising bazaars were organized by and for women, where handcrafts would be created and sold, often bearing anti-slavery slogans. Special school lessons and social events and magazines were created for children, and they were organized to collect pennies to prepare for the day when those in bondage might go free.

The vast majority of active abolitionists were volunteers and part-timers. They were busy with jobs and family responsibilities, and had to grab opportunities for informing and captivating the wider public whenever and wherever they came along. They chimed in at church meetings and business gatherings. Chapter leaders were asked to collect and send in the names of "inquiring, candid, reading men who are not abolitionists" so that these candidates could be mailed persuasive materials. Special efforts were made to reach ministers and enlighten them on issues surrounding slavery, on the grounds that "ministers are the hinges of community, and ought to be moved." Calling on local ministers in person was one of the important duties of the roving lecturers that the AASS hired as agents working across the country.

While Lewis Tappan was the main supervisor of the printed publications that gave the AASS its intellectual backbone, Arthur Tappan was officially in charge of the lecture agents. Both men became quite good at uncovering and recruiting talented thinkers and arguers to work as writers, editors, or speakers. Many abolitionists became convinced in the mid-1830s that the roving agent-lecturers were the most important element in their campaign, on account of their ability to reach the rural masses. Though he was himself an editor of several of the abolitionist journals, mathematician Elizur Wright believed that living, spoken words were even more important than written words at reaching "the country places" that were the key to abolitionist success. "The great cities we cannot expect to carry till the country is won," he concluded. Repeatedly, farmers and the agricultural population rose up to protect abolitionists threatened by urban mobs, and "no city proved in future years as strong in abolition sentiment as rural areas," as historian Whitney Cross put it.

Donors paid for a massive Mississippi Valley Campaign that flooded our frontier Midwest with circuit preachers, public speakers, Sunday-school teachers, and others bearing messages of Christian uplift as well as opposition to human bondage.

The Oberlin Rescuers.
At Cuyahoga Co. jail. April 1859.

Arthur Tappan personally built Oberlin College from nothing into an excellent school and hotbed of social reform. In 1858, a group of Oberlin students and administrators freed an escaped slave who had been snatched up in town by slave catchers. He was sheltered in the home of the college president for several days, then spirited away, causing 21 Oberlin men to be jailed for three months for resisting the Fugitive Slave Law. They were visited in lock-up by hundreds of sympathizers, including Sunday-school children, and published their own newspaper with donated funds while behind bars—creating a bonanza of sympathetic coverage of the abolitionist cause.

The donor-funded Mississippi Valley Campaign turned our Midwest into an anti-slavery bastion. This cultural metamorphosis could later be seen in the avenging actions of William Sherman's western army during the Civil War.

Betting on middle America

As mentioned, the Tappans built up a network of evangelical churches in New York City which they hoped could become a power-pack for abolition and other types of social reform. They had some success in this, creating large and active congregations of prosperous individuals, featuring young men's societies, female auxiliaries, and some impressive pastors. But even in the city, it was discovered, the men and women most devoted to the anti-slavery cause were transplanted country people.

Building on this lesson, Arthur Tappan and other philanthropists became passionate advocates for a push to build reform energy among rural people living along our nation's western frontier (which at that point included the states and territories stretching from Missouri up to the Wisconsin region, then east to Ohio). Arthur was a heavy funder of this effort to bring evangelical culture to a vast swath of land that was fast filling up with the next generation of Americans. This became known as the Mississippi Valley Campaign.

Cincinnati—the "London of the West"—was initially picked as the regional headquarters, and Arthur hired an impressive group of evangelizers, thinkers, writers, and speakers to relocate there and set to work. These included Lyman Beecher, Theodore Weld, and Charles Finney. Arthur thought of these as the movement's "best generals" who "should occupy the very seat of Western warfare." Extensive work was also done down in the trenches. A mechanics' lyceum, Sunday schools, lending libraries, and evening classes were established to spread literacy and new ideas to laborers, farmers, and free blacks. Prayer sessions and sermon series were organized. Schoolteachers were transported from the East, and publications of all sorts were circulated.

Parts of the Cincinnati establishment, however, were scandalized by the mixing of races these activities encouraged, and the activists were chased out of the city. Very quickly, the center of Western abolitionism shifted to the new college Arthur Tappan had established in 1833 at Oberlin, Ohio. Tappan wooed Charles Finney to run the new institution, and poured his personal funds into building it up. "If you will go to Oberlin and take hold of the work," he told Finney, "I will pledge myself to give my entire income, except what I want to provide for my family, till you are beyond pecuniary want."

Arthur Tappan annually put tens of thousands of dollars into Oberlin for years. Soon, it was not only a well-functioning college but a kind of training academy for activists who subsequently fanned out all across the developing American heartland. "Oberlinites spread an influence, 'unseen and unsuspected,' over the Western Reserve and in hundreds of Western communities," summarized Wyatt-Brown. From that moment, the area we now call our Midwest became tightly allied to upstate New York and New England as the heat- and power-generating reactors of abolitionism. The avenging actions of William Sherman's Midwestern army during the Civil War were one later sign of this cultural metamorphosis.

Legal defense

A final technique of the Tappan organizational genius was their marshaling of important legal-defense efforts. By this means they were able to protect pioneer activists. They established vital precedents in courtrooms. And they used high-profile proceedings to educate Americans on the realities of slavery and get them involved in righting the wrong.

Arthur Tappan's first foray into legal defense came in 1830. Very early in his career as an abolitionist

Lewis Tappan almost singlehandedly orchestrated the *Amistad* courtroom struggle into widespread revulsion against slavery. Abolition turned a huge corner toward a wide popular following for the very first time.

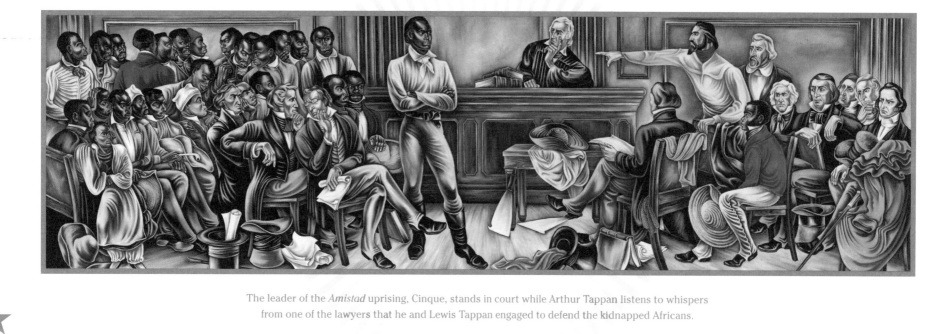

The leader of the *Amistad* uprising, Cinque, stands in court while Arthur Tappan listens to whispers from one of the lawyers that he and Lewis Tappan engaged to defend the kidnapped Africans.

publisher, some of William Lloyd Garrison's reporting on the trade in slaves within the U.S. got him sued for libel by a shipowner, and convicted of criminal charges by the state of Maryland. Garrison was sent to jail for six months. When Tappan heard of his travail, he paid Garrison's fine and court costs, and got him released after seven weeks behind bars. He then gave the editor $100 to help him set up a new weekly anti-slavery newspaper called the *Liberator*. These were the first of many subsidies Arthur provided to the reformer.

Arthur also got involved in a legal case in 1833, in defense of a Connecticut schoolmistress who enrolled a black girl in one of her classes, only to have the state legislature pass a law shutting down her school. Not wanting this precedent to become established in New England jurisprudence, Tappan wrote to offer unconditional support: "Consider me your banker. Spare no necessary expense. Command the services of the ablest lawyers." Upon appeal to the Connecticut Supreme Court, the schoolmistress won her case

(though public pressure forced her to close nonetheless).

The most dramatic Tappan courtroom drama began to unfold in 1839. Though the British Navy was then enforcing a ban on the international slave trade, rogue slavers continued to run Africans into the Americas—sometimes protected by false papers supplied by corrupt U.S. or foreign government officials, assistance from Southerners, and the indifference of much of the American public. Several dozen Africans recently kidnapped from the nation of Sierra

Leone were being transferred across Cuba in a ship called *La Amistad* when the captives took over the ship, killed the captain, and ordered remaining crew members to sail them back to Africa. Instead, the navigators landed the ship near Long Island. The Africans were taken into custody and charged with murder.

As soon as he heard of the case, Lewis Tappan leapt into action. He scoured the New York docks and found a cabin boy who could speak the dialect of the defendants; he was hired to serve as translator. Lewis clothed and fed the prisoners with his own money and donations from other abolitionists. While they were held in New Haven, Lewis arranged for Yale students to tutor the Africans in English, American social practice, and Christianity. He engaged a first-rate legal team to defend them in court. And he launched a journalistic and public-relations effort to use the case as a teachable moment for informing Americans on the realities of slavery.

It took two years for the case to wend its way though the courts. Amidst many legal twists, the case became a national and international cause célèbre, drawing large crowds and banner headlines over many months. As in their great mailing campaign a few years earlier, the Tappans had to battle a U.S. President and the weight of the federal government—lower-court verdicts exonerating the Africans were appealed all the way to the U.S. Supreme Court by Martin Van Buren (spurred by Southern interests). At that point, Lewis Tappan convinced former President John Quincy Adams to join the all-star legal team for the final appeal. Our highest court ultimately ruled that the Africans were kidnap victims, not property, with a right to defend themselves. They were declared wholly free.

Lewis Tappan had almost single-handedly orchestrated this defense (on an entirely volunteer basis, while continuing to attend to his business responsibilities). He engineered the communications and reporting that transfixed many Americans. He hired the legal horses. He attended every day the courts were in session. Some months later he raised the donations needed to return the Africans to their native lands. "The captives are free…thanks in the name of humanity and justice to you," wrote Adams to Tappan after the trial.

"By some peculiar alchemy, Tappan had made the *Amistad* case a 'safe' cause," comments Wyatt-Brown. All across America, the courtroom struggle aroused revulsion against the victimization of innocents. "Such bloodhound persecutions of poor defenseless strangers cast upon the shores should call down the manly and scorching rebukes of universal civilized man," concluded one Ohioan. New disgust with human bondage, mistrust of government and sectional apologists for slavery, sympathy for those held in captivity, and appreciation for freedom fighters erupted across the country. Thousands of people donated money. More subscribed to journals making arguments against

enslavement. Abolition turned a huge corner, for the first time, toward a wide popular following.

The most consequential social change in the history of the United States had begun. And two philanthropist brothers were at the center of it. Combining abundant generosity with high principle, personal passion, and a genius for organizing, they powered a national tide shift that would never be reversed.

Philanthropists who fueled the abolitionist charities recruited highly talented activists to run their journals, organize their societies, and create inspiring art. Poet John Greenleaf Whittier was one of these creative masterminds. Here is the first publication of his poem "Our Countrymen in Chains." The violence at the Chatham Street Chapel that grew into the 1834 anti-abolition riots was sparked by hymn-singing of some of Whittier's verse.

— A CASE STUDY —

Changing Society through Civil Action

Temperance

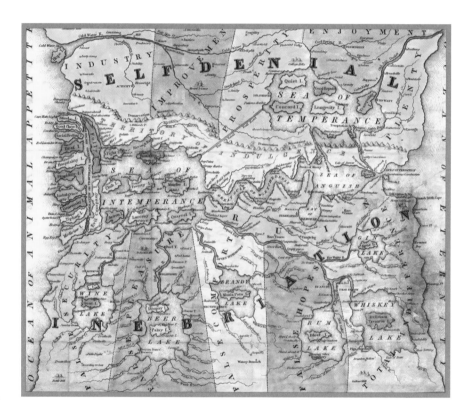

A whimsical 1838 temperance map created by a Philadelphia activist juxtaposes regions of ruin with places of prosperity. Colorful, intricate illustrations like this were often used by social reformers to entertain while instructing and making a point. Think YouTube for a pre-electronic age.

AGAINST PROHIBITION NO. 2.
Lager's amber Fluid mild,
Gives health and strength to wife and child

AGAINST PROHIBITION NO. 3.
The youngster, ruddy with good cheer,
Serenely sips his Lager Beer

America's heavy consumption of alcohol didn't just happen. Booze was heavily promoted by brewers and distillers, even to the young in startling ways.

Right from colonial times, many Americans were concerned that heavy alcohol consumption in our country was fueling crime, poverty, family neglect, lost work, violence, and other social problems. Charitable action to temper alcohol use emerged after the War of 1812, amidst worries about the discipline and industriousness of everyday citizens in our young democracy.

This first effort peaked in the mid-1800s—when close to half of all states put into effect full or partial bans on alcoholic beverages. After the Civil War, America's temperance movement gathered momentum again, culminating in a national ban on selling intoxicants that was put into effect from 1920 to 1933 by Constitutional amendment. While government prohibition ultimately failed, the multi-generational civil movement to encourage more temperate use of alcohol was profoundly successful in changing America.

An alcoholic haze

"Americans drank from the crack of dawn to the crack of dawn." That's how one historian described the 1800s. That an alcoholic haze hung over many of our communities is backed up by hard numbers. In 1823, the average adult American imbibed seven and a half gallons of alcohol each year. This is the equivalent, notes author Daniel Okrent, of consuming more than a bottle and a half of standard 80-proof liquor, per adult, *every single week*. In the early decades of the nineteenth century, more money was spent on alcoholic drinks than the total expenditure of the national government.

In 1890, San Francisco hosted one saloon for every 58

Violence carried out by drunken husbands and fathers spurred many women to become involved in campaigns to moderate alcohol use.

"Americans drank from the crack of dawn to the crack of dawn."

residents—counting men, women, and children. That same year, Jacob Riis counted saloons in Manhattan for his book *How the Other Half Lives*. Just in the area south of 14th Street, which was packed with poor immigrants, he found 4,065 booze shops. (The same district was home to 111 churches.) Riis described how drunkard parents would send their children to bars with a tin pail to have it filled with beer. They coated their buckets with lard on the inside to keep the foam down and maximize the quantity of lager received.

Reform schools and workhouses were filled with heavy drinkers. An 1833 survey of the inmates of Auburn Prison found that 57 percent had been drunk when they committed the crime they were incarcerated for. Three quarters of the men admitted to being habitual heavy drinkers.

Plenty of propaganda and exploitation went into building up this level of drinking. The president of one of the distiller associations pressed Congress to give liquor to soldiers to "insure the steadiness of nerve that wins battles.... The man who rushes a rapid-fire gun should be given the relief from terror that alcohol imparts." Cheap gin was created specifically to be marketed to impoverished blacks in the South at fifty cents per pint. Children were directly taken advantage of. Speaking at one distillers' meeting, a dealer urged that "we must create the appetite for liquor in the growing boys.... Nickels expended in treats to boys now will return in dollars to your tills after the appetite has been formed." Brewers pushed the idea that beer was "healthful," and that it would calm children. (See period advertisements nearby.)

In addition to damaged health, family turmoil, workplace costs, and other nasty social fallout, the high rate of alcohol consumption degraded American politics. Brewers and distillers spent large amounts of money to buy votes, influence elections, bribe journalists, and so forth. The saloon became the headquarters for corrupt machine politics. In 1884, fully half of the members of New York City's board of aldermen were saloonkeepers, and a third of the others owed their posts to backing by saloon owners. A worker at a charity that helped immigrants in Boston said that "the affiliation between the saloon and politics was so close that for all practical purposes the two might have been under one and the same control." Selling your vote for the price of a day's bar tab was very common.

Close-up on two groups of activists: women and entrepreneurs

Stepping up to battle the problems that resulted from heavy alcohol use were a series of volunteer and charitable organizations: the American Temperance Society, the Temperance Union, Washingtonian Societies, the Order of the Sons of Temperance, the Women's Christian Temperance Union, the Anti-Saloon League, and many others. Three main categories of Americans drove the temperance movement: 1) evangelical Christians acting as part of their larger commitment to improve human life through benevolent service, 2) reformist business entrepreneurs fired by a vision of national progress through personal industry and social improvement, and 3) women.

Daniel Okrent notes that women were often indirect and entirely innocent victims of alcohol:

A drunken husband and father was sufficient cause for pain, but many women also had to endure the associated ravages born of the early saloon: the wallet emptied into a bottle, the job lost or farmwork left undone, and most pitilessly… venereal disease contracted by the wives of drink-sodden husbands who had found something more than liquor lurking in saloons.

Women traumatized by alcohol discovered how vulnerable they were on many levels. They wanted saloons regulated, but they also needed action on other fronts.

They wanted the right to own property, and to shield their families' financial security from the profligacy of drunken husbands. They wanted the right to divorce those men, and to have them arrested for wife beating, and to protect their children from being terrorized.

The leading appeal made by the Women's Christian Temperance Union was "Home Protection." That was broadly popular. And it fed the appetite for voting rights for women. Many suffragists, including

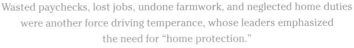

Wasted paychecks, lost jobs, undone farmwork, and neglected home duties were another force driving temperance, whose leaders emphasized the need for "home protection."

On one of New York City's skid rows, two men sleep off a binge.

Activist businessmen who resembled and foreshadowed today's entrepreneurial philanthropists took important roles in reducing alcohol abuse.

Amelia Bloomer, Elizabeth Cady Stanton, Lucy Stone, and Susan B. Anthony began their public lives as temperance activists and shifted to voting rights after. It is no accident that our Constitution's Nineteenth Amendment enfranchising women was ratified exactly one year after the Eighteenth Amendment banished most alcohol sales.

Self-made businessmen were another major force behind the temperance drive, both as organizers and as funders. In many fascinating ways, these activist entrepreneurs resemble and foreshadow the entrepreneurial philanthropists who are so influential in civic reform today. Based on close study of the individuals who led and donated money to the civil movement against alcohol, scholar Ian Tyrrell reports that these Americans were

not the reactionary, provincial movement of popular belief.... On the contrary, temperance reformers...optimistically predicted the improvement of the moral state of society.... They were men who were working to create

a society of competitive individuals instilled with the virtues of sobriety and industry.... They were excited by the economic progress and vast potential of the United States. Because the nation's character was still being forged, temperance reformers believed that they had a unique opportunity to shape the future.

It's natural that economic strivers and improvers would be interested in temperance. And mass drunkenness was an obvious problem. More than three quarters of the 7,000 business leaders who answered an official questionnaire in 1897 expressed concern about alcohol abuse among their employees.

Many of the public-spirited businessmen trying to change drinking habits were the same ones involved in creating public libraries, mechanics institutes, worker lyceums, and YMCAs. They wanted to encourage self-improvement, moral refinement, and education among laborers. And they believed that modern organizing (such as the new charitable groups) and modern technology (like steam-powered printing presses) offered fresh ways of enlightening individuals and strengthening society.

Like many current entrepreneurs who turn to philanthropy to improve American life, the business leaders taking part in the temperance movement often expressed dual motivations. One was a sense of their own rising influence and responsibilities. A second impulse came from their unease that hundreds of thousands of fellow citizens lived miserably in a land of great richness. These yielded an "urge to transform the moral condition of society," as Tyrrell puts it. And these men were "prepared to disrupt the social order to achieve their ends."

Edward Delavan was a self-made businessman who made a fortune in the hardware trade in the 1820s. He then retired on his investments at an early age and devoted himself to what he called "the improvement of mankind." He was religious, as well as an idealistic advocate of practical progress. He became the influential secretary of the New York State Temperance Society, and spent 30 years financing

and guiding the movement for sobriety to ever-wider success.

John Cocke, who served as president of the American Temperance Union from 1836 to 1843, and provided funding his whole life long, founded enterprises that smelted copper, and built canals and railroads. His business partner Christian Keener was also an important temperance activist, and the chief donor to the Maryland Temperance Society. Anson Phelps, also in mining and smelting, was one of the wealthiest industrialists in the country, and a major temperance supporter. George Odiorne was an advanced iron manufacturer and wealthy banker who gave loyally of both money and time.

Matthias Baldwin was a technologist who became wealthy after greatly improving the design of locomotives. Wholly self-made, he viewed his temperance philanthropy as one of the best ways he could help others discipline and improve themselves and follow him into success. Daniel Fanshaw was an improver of the printing process in America. He directly applied his skills in modern communications on behalf of the New York City Temperance Society.

During the nineteenth century, the temperance movement relied most of all on persuasion, peer support, and voluntary pledges to moderate or stop alcohol use.

Fraternal organizations, spontaneous grassroots support groups like the Washingtonian societies, and specialized private businesses sprang up to help fellow citizens keep clean and sober.

Three Tappan brothers—not only the well-known Arthur and Lewis but also brother John, who served on the executive board of the American Temperance Society—ranked for years among the top bankrollers of temperance organizing. Like most of the others I have just cited, the Tappans were highly innovative in the ways they made their money. And moral considerations were important not only in their philanthropy but also in their business practices. Lewis's creation of the first system for rating the credit-worthiness of businesses and businessmen, for instance, was important in cleaning up the world of finance, and introducing rational moral considerations into commerce.

Many more such world-changing businessmen put energy into the temperance crusade—right up to John Rockefeller, who, in addition to being America's most successful business creator ever, was a lifelong Baptist and a teetotaler. He was a steadfast financial supporter of the Anti-Saloon League. Rockefeller would match with an additional 10 percent from his own pocket whatever the ASL was able to raise from donors every year.

The temperance philanthropists believed that alleviating problem-drinking would require individual transformation. But they also thought it required societal change. They wanted to speed both kinds of reform. Opposing them was much of the establishment. Lawyers, old money, settled merchants, non-evangelical clergy, and defenders of the status quo mostly discounted the temperance vision for a better life, or actively fought it.

A multipronged attempt to persuade

The civil-action portion of the anti-alcohol campaign (before it turned into a Constitutional amendment) was built on *persuasion*. It became a multimedia effort, propelled by millions of published words, the most popular public speakers of the day, school curricula pumped across the country, prominent blue-ribbon commissions, celebrity endorsements, popular songs and entertainments. It involved one of the widest coalitions ever assembled for social change, running from unionists to manufacturers, political conservatives to avowed radicals, rural pastors to urban settlement-house activists, very rich to very poor. There were charitable groups working to change conditions at every level: nationally, in states and counties, within workplaces, through individuals signing personal pledges. In many of these undertakings, temperance went from strength to strength, meeting disappointment only when it devolved into federal command and control.

Abraham Lincoln was a supporter. In an 1842 speech he said "the temperance revolution" could break individual "bondage" and "slavery" of the most tyrannical sort, and offer "more of want supplied, more disease healed, more sorrow assuaged" than nearly any other social reform. He expressed excitement that "the cause itself seems suddenly transformed from a cold abstract theory to a living, breathing, active, and powerful" force.

Lincoln was particularly appreciative that temperance proponents were relying on empathetic argument. "When the conduct of men is designed to be influenced," he urged, "persuasion, kind unassuming persuasion, should ever be adopted." The anti-alcohol persuaders he admired understood that problem drinkers were often "their old friends and companions. They know they are not demons." So the campaigners engaged as "practical philanthropists, and they glow with a generous and brotherly zeal."

These empathetic activists first sought moderation. And even for the alcohol-addicted they called not for laws or sentences but for individual pledges of abstinence—backed and made workable by a whole architecture of peer support, familiar to anyone today who knows how Alcoholics Anonymous works. Reasoning, education, and mutual reinforcement were the main tools.

As early as the 1830s, the New York State Temperance Society, one of the first state-level charities to become active, was printing 12 million pieces of literature every year—and actually *selling* enough of them to cover more than two thirds of its annual expenses. The Anti-Saloon League produced ten tons of printed matter *per day* at its Ohio press in 1916. Its annual budget that year, in today's dollars, was $57 million.

Essay contests on the damage done by alcohol were launched with substantial prizes. These attracted broad notice and many entries, and winning

This fountain, still standing in downtown D.C., was one of many built by temperance donors—in practical recognition that if people couldn't find convenient, sanitary drinking sources in public they would end up in taverns.

The cause became extremely popular, and produced some of the mightiest culture-change organizations in American history. Neighborhood life saw marked reductions in disorder, family quarrels, and abusive behavior.

stories were widely read once published. Doctors were also recruited to sign statements on the unhealthfulness of distilled spirits, and medical societies were enlisted in campaigns.

From its very beginning, the temperance movement worked hard to reach young people. Early anti-alcohol societies sprang up at colleges like Amherst, Williams, Union, Andover, and Colgate. Eventually, detailed lessons were created for primary and secondary schools. By the end of the 1800s, temperance education was part of weekly instruction for children and teenagers in every U.S. state.

Fraternal organizations were created to offer social life, mutual support, and benefits like insurance to Americans who favored temperance. The Sons of Temperance, founded in 1842, had a quarter of a million paying members by 1850. The Cadets of Temperance, Good Samaritans, Band of Hope, and others provided similar offerings, including special fraternities for young people, women, and blacks.

Moderation in all things

Through most of their 100-year history, temperance forces were more focused on self-regulation and local decision-making than on totalist national edicts. Up through the mid-1800s, the emphasis was very much on individual conversion, and personal pledges of moderation or abstinence.

"The first time I heard in America that 100,000 men had publicly promised never to drink alcohol liquor, I thought it more of a joke than a serious matter," wrote Frenchman Alexis de Tocqueville in his 1835 travelogue *Democracy in America*. But he later marveled that this was a sincere action to encourage others through example rather than control. "In the end I came to understand that these hundred thousand Americans, frightened by the progress of drunkenness around them, wanted to support sobriety by their patronage…. If they had lived in France, each of these hundred thousand would have made individual representations to the government asking it to supervise all the public houses throughout the realm."

Convinced that plenty of Americans entered taverns simply because it could be hard to wet one's whistle in any other way when out in public,

The campaign against alcohol abuse was a grand coalition that united people from vastly disparate backgrounds. Supporters included Frederick Douglass (1), Booker T. Washington (2), Jane Addams (3), Orville Wright (4), Billy Sunday (5), Philip Randolph, William Jennings Bryan, Susan B. Anthony, Upton Sinclair, Booth Tarkington, and many others.

temperance donors paid for the construction of drinking fountains in many cities. Some were quite elaborate, or sentimental, or didactic, or attracted people in some other way. An example that still stands in Washington, D.C., in a prominent spot just off Pennsylvania Avenue, was one of many built by Henry Cogswell, a San Francisco millionaire. It became popular because it was designed to hold ice in a reservoir under its base— and thus dispensed chilled

water to any passerby even in hot weather. (The piping was eventually disconnected when the city government got tired of replenishing the ice supply.)

America's first strict limits on alcohol peddling came through democratic action, a full lifetime before national prohibition, when Maine voted for statewide limits on sales starting in 1846. By 1855, another 14 states had decided to join Maine in blocking sales of intoxicating beverages, and Pennsylvania and New Jersey

both fell one legislative vote short. More than a half-century later, one of the primary goals of even the hardball-playing Anti-Saloon League was simply to let various communities choose for themselves what they would allow in alcohol sales. There was a push for "local-option bills" that let residents decide on a place-by-place basis whether they would be wet or dry.

This democratic, non-utopian, non-coercive approach reflected a willingness to be satisfied just

with reclaiming one's own sphere of life, without pressing overly hard on others. You can glimpse that spirit in a letter from John Noyes: "What if there is not another bright spot in the wide world, and what if ours is a very small one? Turn your eye toward it when you are tired of looking into chaos, and you will catch a glimpse of a better world." In that bit of modest, human-scale wisdom there is a lesson for philanthropic reformers of today as well.

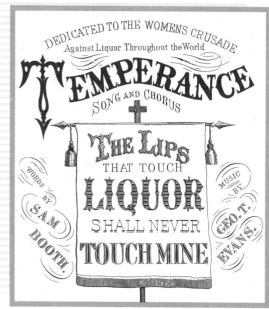

Recognizing that "feelings of sociality" drew many people into taverns, temperance organizers created a culture of songs, social gatherings, fairs, and parades to attract supporters.

Human sparkplugs

Temperance built a large cadre of creative, energetic, and determined leaders. Francis Willard was the first dean of women at Northwestern University before she founded the Women's Christian Temperance Union. There she became, as Susan B. Anthony once said, "the commander-in-chief of an army of 250,000 women" (who she sometimes referred to as her "Protestant nuns").

Before he became the sparkplug of the Anti-Saloon League, Wayne Wheeler was aptly described by a classmate as a "locomotive in trousers." If he had actually been made of steel, though, he might never have turned his energy to temperance. A formative early experience was having a hayfork lodged in his leg by a blind-drunk laborer at his family farm.

Another "father" of the movement was Richmond Hobson. You can get a sense of the energy he brought to the cause from a little excerpt from one of his convention addresses in 1915. He called on fellow agitators to mail out "speeches and other documents. Request all papers and periodicals to decline liquor advertisements. Call the Salvation Army into action. Develop local fights so as to produce the best effect on the national field. Take the offensive everywhere. Attack! Attack! Attack!"

Temperance activists stirred up voluntary boycotts which convinced the *New York Tribune, Boston Record, Chicago Herald*, and other newspapers to stop accepting liquor advertisements. Protestant churches organized a vast number of public events, and supplied clergy and volunteers from their congregations to staff them. A "Committee of Fourteen" united a range of prominent citizens in an effort to close loopholes that allowed some saloons to skirt laws blocking liquor sales on Sundays. A different "Committee of Fifty" was organized by academics and lawyers to take a look at alcohol and temperance; their report had aimed to draw a line down the middle, yet caused Harvard president Charles Eliot to forswear even the mild imbibing he had long practiced. He became an abstainer instead.

Temperance forces recruited prominent international humanitarians like Leo Tolstoy and British philanthropist Isabella Somerset in support of their cause. A great many abolitionists and black leaders, including Frederick Douglass, Wendell Phillips, William Lloyd Garrison, Neal Dow, and Booker T. Washington, lent their endorsements, arguing that heavy alcohol was a special scourge among African-Americans, creating "a different form of slavery." Yale economist Irving Fisher organized a group of famous Americans who agreed on little else except that alcohol overuse was a plague. It included individuals like inventor Orville Wright, novelist Booth Tarkington, the chairman of U.S. Steel, and rabble-rouser Upton Sinclair.

In these days before radio and TV, public speaking was a crucial element of any campaign to change the nation's direction. One of the early popular speakers was John Gough, a reformed drinker and former actor. During his career, he delivered more than 10,000 temperance speeches heard by an estimated 9 million Americans. Former drunkard John Hawkins, a hatter by trade, traveled 200,000 miles after his retirement to deliver testimonials. Three-time Presidential candidate William Jennings Bryan was an influential

anti-alcohol barnstormer. He delivered hundreds of addresses every year, often to large crowds. After one talk to 20,000 people in Philadelphia, 12,000 members of the audience took a pledge of total abstinence. Richmond Hobson was another popular orator. In addition to those who heard him, an estimated 2 million printed copies of his "Great Destroyer" speech were distributed to the public.

Billy Sunday was a professional baseball player turned preacher whose colorful railing against alcohol abuse drew a huge following. He knew his subject—brewers and distillers owned most of the early professional baseball teams, and the stadiums were drenched in beer and whiskey. The tickets sold to fans often included two drinks at the "booze cages" that dominated lower seating areas. Many players became alcoholics. Billy Sunday attracted crowds of 10,000 listeners and more to his enormous touring tent. During his 40 years of speaking up to 250 times per year, more than 100 million Americans took in at least one of his manic addresses.

"I will fight them until hell freezes over," he said of alcohol

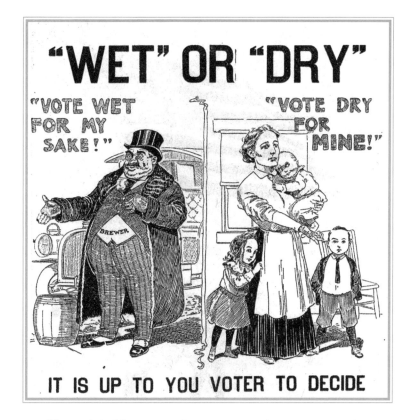

When it shifted from personal persuasion to policy campaigning, the temperance movement was highly democratic, and pushed mostly for "local-option bills" that let residents decide on a place-by-place basis whether their town, county, or state would traffic in alcohol.

THE AMERICAN ISSUE

A Saloonless Nation and a Stainless Flag

Volume XXVI   WESTERVILLE, OHIO, JANUARY 25, 1919   Number 4

U.S. IS VOTED DRY

36th STATE RATIFIES DRY AMENDMENT JAN. 16

Nebraska Noses Out Missouri for Honor of Completing Job of Writing Dry Act Into the Constitution; Wyoming, Wisconsin and Minnesota Right on Their Heels

JANUARY 16, 1919, MOMENTOUS DAY IN WORLD'S HISTORY

Prohibition was not a coup d'etat by bluenoses, it was a huge popular swell. More than 80 percent of the nation's state legislators voted in favor of a dry nation.

The decades of prayer, persuasion, protest, printed matter, and peer support, the exuberant examples, editorials, education, and electioneering, the sweet singalongs, self-help confessions, and school lessons, the railing, rallying, and referenda— eventually these efforts told.

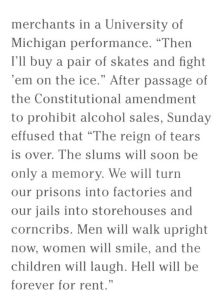

merchants in a University of Michigan performance. "Then I'll buy a pair of skates and fight 'em on the ice." After passage of the Constitutional amendment to prohibit alcohol sales, Sunday effused that "The reign of tears is over. The slums will soon be only a memory. We will turn our prisons into factories and our jails into storehouses and corncribs. Men will walk upright now, women will smile, and the children will laugh. Hell will be forever for rent."

A grand coalition

The coalition of groups and individuals that voluntarily drew together to tamp down alcohol abuse was one of the broadest in the history of American social movements. In addition to the evangelical Christians, women, and business entrepreneurs whose practical and moral concerns gave the effort its deepest energy, there were many on the left who agreed something needed to be done.

Lillian Wald, who brought nursing, improved hygiene, and better family life to squalid tenements in New York City, was a backer. Jane Addams, Jacob Riis, and other progressives were disturbed by the damage done to the poor by alcohol. African-American union organizer Philip Randolph later argued that throttling back alcohol use would bring higher wages, less corrupt politics, lower crime rates, and other good results. Drink only befogged and numbed workers in ways that hurt their best interests, argued a variety of socialist groups.

One of the most remarkable aspects of the campaign against heavy drinking was its success in crossing and uniting economic classes. While the first seeds of backlash were planted by educated clergy and successful civic leaders, the main force that brought the temperance effort to its peak before the Civil War was a spontaneous rising of artisans and manual workers. The so-called Washingtonian movement began in 1840 in a rude Baltimore tavern, where six casual drinkers began to rue their dependence on whiskey. They took a mutual pledge to help each other walk away from liquor, naming their effort in admiration of the self-discipline shown by the father of our nation, and with the idea that just as Washington had defeated political oppression, so could the oppression of "both body and mind" imposed by the "tyrant" alcohol be beaten.

The society they formed spread like wildfire among the working class. Within a few years the movement had hundreds of thousands of adherents across the major Northern cities. Chapters were organized to offer tradesmen, laborers, and artisans a solidarity group to lean on. There were branches for bakers, printers, carters, butchers, sailors, firemen, hatters, carpenters, shipwrights, and caulkers. Washingtonian societies formed to support abstinence along the docks, in slums, within prisons, and among released felons. It was a remarkable, self-organizing effort "by drunkards for drunkards," all seeking a better life. And it created a proletarian infantry that meshed powerfully with the church ladies and business owners and community leaders who formed the artillery. That was the united social force that resulted in 15 of 31 U.S. states making themselves fully or nearly dry within little more than a decade.

The desire to make their campaign a popular one drew temperance campaigners into the world of entertainment. Popular celebrities were recruited to endorse the cause. There were temperance balls, fairs, musical

events, and parades. As early as the 1840s, temperance concerts were drawing crowds of 4,000 people or more.

Movement leaders noted that "man is a social being" and that "love of company" and "feelings of sociality" were the forces that drew many Americans into taverns. So alternative social life was provided. Singing became a big part of gatherings. Many original songs and hymns were written, and temperance "glee singers" made merry with ditties like "Blue Monday," "I've Thrown

the Bowl Aside," and "Close Up the Booze Shop."

The triumph beneath the flop
Because today's conventional wisdom is that alcoholic prohibition was nothing but a puritanical flop, it needs to be pointed out that the movement was both extremely popular in its day and powerful in its ultimate effects. As early as 1833, more than 700 separate Temperance Society branches had been organized in our largest state (New York). Fully 133 out of 292

A spontaneous anti-alcohol effort among manual workers —by drunkards for drunkards— created a proletarian infantry that meshed powerfully with the church ladies, business owners, and community leaders who formed the temperance artillery.

93

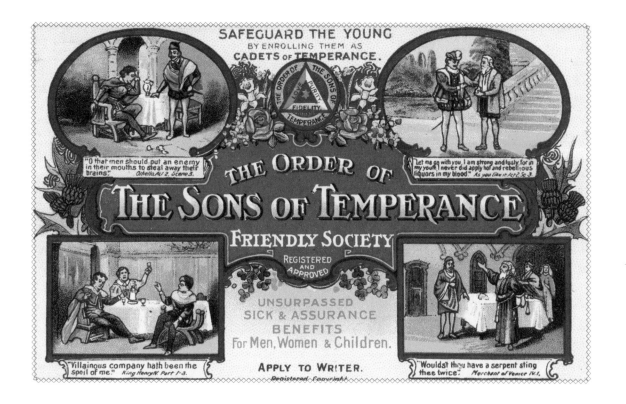

century." When group leader Frances Willard died in 1898, 20,000 people traveled to Chicago on a single day to view her casket.

And overlapping with the WCTU was the Anti-Saloon League—the mightiest culture-change group in America during its decades of operation. For many generations, alcohol manufacturers were America's fifth or sixth largest industry, and a powerful political pressure group. But by 1909 the secretary of the U.S. Brewers' Association was warning his membership that "we have to reckon with" the Anti-Saloon League, which "has over 800 business offices, and at least 500 men and women on its regular salary list…. It employs large numbers of speakers on contract, from the governor of Indiana down to the local pastor of the Methodist Church." Neither before nor since has any group orchestrated an amendment of our Constitution more tidily than the ASL.

Like lots of social movements, the crusade against intoxication eventually went too far. At hotbed Oberlin College, the stigma against alcohol was eventually extended to proscribe stimulants like tea, coffee, gravy, butter, and pepper! And we all know the problems of

distilleries in the state had been closed. And 12 out of every 100 New York residents had signed a pledge of alcoholic abstinence.

By a generation later, when national prohibition was being voted on in the U.S. House of Representatives, a petition was submitted to the chamber which bore 12,000 signatures—these represented not individual Americans but rather *organizations* that were

requesting that alcohol sales be banished. When the prohibition amendment to our Constitution went to the states, more than 80 percent of the nation's state legislators voted dry.

The Women's Christian Temperance Union has faded from modern memories. Historians, though, refer to the charity as "the nation's most effective political action group in the last decades of the nineteenth enforcement and government over-reach that eventually doomed the national prohibition against alcohol production.

But that is not the end of the story. The decades of prayer, persuasion, printed matter, protest, and peer support, the exuberant examples, editorials, education, and electioneering, the sweet singalongs, self-help confessions, and school lessons, the railing, rallying, and referenda—eventually these efforts told. The children and grandchildren of Washingtonians decided that alcoholic bingeing wasn't fun. The famous *Middletown* sociology study showed that when social leaders in heartland towns decided to stop drinking, many other Americans were influenced.

Decades of civil organizing throttled back booze consumption from our frontier-era average of 7.5 gallons of alcohol per adult per year all the way down to 2.6 gallons by the early 1900s. During the first few years of national prohibition, drinking fell 70 percent more, and arrests for public drunkenness tumbled, as did alcohol-related deaths. Chicago closed one of its jails, Grand Rapids abandoned its

work farm, church membership in the U.S. rose by 1.2 million, and Jane Addams described "the marked decrease" in disorderly conduct, street fights, family quarrels, and abuse in poor neighborhoods.

As the years went on, bootleggers innovated, enforcement sagged, and drinking rebounded some. Yet even after repeal, alcohol consumption in the U.S. remained about 30 percent below its pre-prohibition level. Today, American alcohol consumption is about 2.2 gallons per adult per year. That's a 71 percent reduction from when the temperance activists first went to work.

More fundamentally, a new ethic of responsibility and seriousness took root in America. "The temperance movement," summarizes historian Ian Tyrrell, "profoundly influenced American values."

Reform helped to popularize the idea of self-improvement and strengthened the bourgeois ethic of frugality, sobriety, and industry in American society. Until the 1830s, Americans saw no

Though conventionally viewed as a flop, the temperance movement actually reduced alcohol consumption dramatically—to just 29 percent, today, of the levels when reformers went to work. And then there's their influence on wider American values...

necessary link between temperance, respectability, and self-improvement; as a result of temperance agitation, middle-class culture and all who aspired to middle-class status would be deeply influenced.

This transformation was driven by volunteers and donors—men and women pursuing the national interest, but more often through philanthropy than politics.

About The Philanthropy Roundtable

The Philanthropy Roundtable is America's leading network of charitable donors working to strengthen our free society, uphold donor intent, and protect the freedom to give. Our members include individual philanthropists, families, corporations, and private foundations.

Mission

The Philanthropy Roundtable's mission is to foster excellence in philanthropy, to protect philanthropic freedom, to assist donors in achieving their philanthropic intent, and to help donors advance liberty, opportunity, and personal responsibility in America and abroad.

Principles

- Philanthropic freedom is essential to a free society
- A vibrant private sector generates the wealth that makes philanthropy possible
- Voluntary private action offers solutions to many of society's most pressing challenges
- Excellence in philanthropy is measured by results, not by good intentions
- A respect for donor intent is essential to long-term philanthropic success

Services

World-class conferences

The Philanthropy Roundtable connects you with other savvy donors. Held across the nation throughout the year, our meetings assemble grantmakers and experts to develop strategies for excellent local, state, and national giving. You will hear from innovators in K–12 education, economic opportunity, higher education, national security, and other fields. Our Annual Meeting is the Roundtable's flagship event, gathering the nation's most public-spirited and influential philanthropists for debates, how-to sessions, and discussions on the best ways for private individuals to achieve powerful results through their giving. The Annual Meeting is a stimulating and enjoyable way to meet principled donors seeking the breakthroughs that can solve our nation's greatest challenges.

Breakthrough groups

Our Breakthrough groups—focused program areas—build a critical mass of donors around a topic where dramatic results are within reach. Breakthrough groups become a springboard to help donors achieve lasting effects from their philanthropy. Our specialized staff of experts helps grantmakers invest with care in areas like anti-poverty work, philanthropy for veterans, and family reinforcement. The Roundtable's K–12 education program is our largest and longest-running Breakthrough group. This network helps donors zero in on today's most promising school reforms. We are the industry-leading convener for philanthropists seeking systemic improvements through competition and parental choice, administrative freedom and accountability, student-centered technology, enhanced teaching and school leadership, and high standards and expectations for students of all backgrounds. We foster productive collaboration among donors of varied ideological perspectives who are united by a devotion to educational excellence.

A powerful voice

The Roundtable's public-policy project, the Alliance for Charitable Reform (ACR), works to advance the principles and preserve the rights of private giving. ACR educates legislators and policymakers about the central role of charitable giving in American life and the crucial importance of protecting philanthropic freedom—the ability of individuals and private organizations to determine how and where to direct their charitable assets. Active in Washington, D.C., and in the states, ACR protects charitable giving, defends the diversity of charitable causes, and battles intrusive government regulation. We believe the capacity of private initiative to address national problems must not be burdened with costly or crippling constraints.

Protection of donor interests

The Philanthropy Roundtable is the leading force in American philanthropy to protect donor intent. Generous givers want assurance that their money will be used for the specific charitable aims and purposes they believe in, not redirected to some other agenda. Unfortunately, donor intent is usually violated in increments, as foundation staff and trustees neglect or misconstrue the founder's values and drift into other purposes. Through education, practical guidance, legislative action, and individual consultation, The Philanthropy Roundtable is active in guarding donor intent. We are happy to advise you on steps you can take to ensure that your mission and goals are protected.

Must-read publications

Philanthropy, the Roundtable's quarterly magazine, is packed with useful and beautifully written real-life stories. It offers practical examples, inspiration, detailed information, history, and clear guidance on the differences between giving that is great and giving that disappoints.

We also publish a series of guidebooks that provide detailed information on the very best ways to be effective in particular aspects of philanthropy. These guidebooks are compact, brisk, and readable. Most focus on one particular area of giving—for instance, how to improve teaching, charter school expansion, support for veterans, programs that get the poor into jobs, how to invest in public policy, and other topics of interest to grantmakers. Real-life examples, hard numbers, first-hand experiences of other donors, recent history, and policy guidance are presented to inform and inspire savvy donors.

The Roundtable's *Almanac of American Philanthropy* is the definitive reference book on private giving in our country. It profiles America's greatest givers (historic and current), describes the 1,000 most consequential philanthropic achievements since our founding, and compiles comprehensive statistics on the field. Our *Almanac* summarizes the major books, key articles, and most potent ideas animating U.S. philanthropy. It includes a 23-page timeline, national poll, legal analysis, and other crucial—and fascinating—finger-tip facts on this vital piece of American culture.

Join the Roundtable!

When working with The Philanthropy Roundtable, members are better equipped to achieve long-lasting success with their charitable giving. Your membership in the Roundtable will make you part of a potent network that understands philanthropy and strengthens our free society. Philanthropy Roundtable members range from Forbes 400 individual givers and the largest American foundations to small family foundations and donors just beginning their charitable careers. Our members include:

- Individuals and families
- Private foundations
- Community foundations
- Venture philanthropists
- Corporate giving programs
- Large operating foundations and charities that devote more than half of their budget to external grants

Philanthropists who contribute at least $100,000 annually to charitable causes are eligible to become members of the Roundtable and register for most of our programs. Roundtable events provide you with a solicitation-free environment.

For more information on The Philanthropy Roundtable or to learn about our individual program areas, please call (202) 822-8333 or e-mail main@PhilanthropyRoundtable.org.

About the Author

Karl Zinsmeister oversees all magazine, book, and website publishing at The Philanthropy Roundtable in Washington, D.C. He also founded and advises the Roundtable's program on philanthropy for veterans and servicemembers. Karl has authored 12 books, including the monumental *Almanac of American Philanthropy* published in 2016, a book on donor funding for public-policy change, a book on philanthropic support of charter schools, two different works of embedded reporting on the Iraq war, a storytelling cookbook, even a graphic novel published by Marvel Comics. He is creator of the "Sweet Charity" podcast, available on iTunes or at SweetCharityPodcast.org. He has made a PBS feature film and written hundreds of articles for publications ranging from the *Atlantic* to the *Wall Street Journal*. Earlier in his career he was a Senate aide to Daniel Patrick Moynihan, then the J. B. Fuqua Fellow at the American Enterprise Institute, and editor in chief for nearly 13 years of *The American Enterprise* magazine. From 2006 to 2009 Karl served in the West Wing as the President's chief domestic policy adviser and director of the White House Domestic Policy Council. He is a graduate of Yale University, and also studied at Trinity College Dublin.